Support Group

Dennis O'Hara and Jules Schwartz

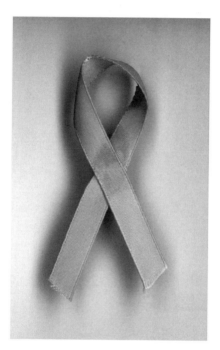

Every disease or cause seems to have a ribbon. This silver ribbon is worn by the men in our support group to promote Prostate Cancer awareness. It was introduced to us by Michael Korda at our annual Cancer Survivor's Day picnic in June of 1996. The American Cancer Society does not yet recognize this.

Disclaimer

This book is intended as an educational tool to acquaint the reader with methods of detecting and treating prostate cancer. The authors hope the book will enable you to improve your well-being and to better assess the available courses of treatment. Many of the alternative methods described have not yet been investigated and approved by a governmental agency. Accordingly, this book should not be substituted for the advice and treatment of a physician or other appropriate licensed health care professional. Because your health is ultimately your responsibility, we hope the information given will enable you to fully participate in any decisions regarding prostate cancer.

Scripture taken from the Holy Bible, New International Version®. Copyright © 1973, 1978, 1984, by International Bible Society. Used by permission of International Bible Society.

"NIV" and "New International Version" are trademarks registered in the United States Patent and Trademark office by International Bible Society

First Edition
Published in the USA by SJDJ Inc.
Copyright © 1997 by Dennis O'Hara & Jules Schwartz SJDJ Inc.
ISBN: 0-9662921-0-3
LCCN: 98-91275
Book design by Christopher O'Hara & Brian O'Hara
Book cover by Christopher O'Hara

"Knowledge equals Survival"

Men, Hit Below the Belt?
PSA rising? Biopsy in your future?
Just diagnosed?
Meet with our survivor support group,
Be educated and encouraged
Make an informed decision
Alleviate the fear

Next meeting Sept. 7 Tuesday
First Tuesday of Every Month 4:30 pm
Convenes at Hurley Reformed Church, Hurley
You'll find friends here

Spouse/significant other welcome
Prostate Cancer 101

www.prostatecancer101.org
Call: (845) 331-7241

Table of Contents

Foreword
Acknowledgements
Introduction

FOREWORD

Most books are written by a professional person, or a professional author. Dennis O'Hara and Jules Schwartz are neither of these. They are two ordinary people, with common sense, who are self educated regarding prostate cancer (PCa). Much of this knowledge comes from the Man to Man support group research and their own personal experiences.

Statistics can be confusing and even depressing. When applied to PCa they can be very cold and impersonal. In this book we relate more to real people in human terms. We can learn a lot from the experiences of the many individual cases outlined in this book.

In a short but informative chapter it is mentioned that there are similarities between PCa and other types of cancer. There are also differences. Each case can be unique and quite different, especially the more advanced cases.

In this disease there is little black and white and so much grey area. This book presents us with many individual stories that anyone can relate to and understand. We are dealing with human beings who have feelings. This book tells how they react under various circumstances.

With over two million cases of PCa and another 200,000 projected for 1998 (figure from American Cancer Society) it's likely that sooner or later almost everyone will know someone (friend or family) who has PCa. This book is loaded with information about a subject where there is plenty of ignorance. The case histories alone provide a vast amount of data.

The focus of "Support Group" is about people like your next door neighbor. Emphasis is on how important it is to be informed and certainly not to depend just on one doctor. Everyday ordinary people, like yourself, are often faced with a dilemma: what treatment to opt for to deal with a disease where there are so many grey areas.

The interviews are proof of how much information can be obtained at a support group meeting. There are even cases where a person's life may have been saved, thanks to something he learned at a Man to Man meeting.

Jules and Dennis have both seen so many men who obtain vital information long after important decisions were made. Many of these men would have taken a different path if they had the knowledge then that they have now. We are confident that this book will result in a lot fewer men making poor decisions.

"Knowledge equals Survival"

ACKNOWLEDGEMENTS

To my best friend who is also my wife Jackie, my children Denise, Jackie and Brian, who put up with a lot of prostate cancer. To all my family and friends who constantly bear with me through my trials and tribulations and are a constant source of comfort. Thank you to all the men in our Man to Man group, both living and deceased and to all the doctors who have cooperated with us. To Jules, who constantly urged me to write this book "Support Group" and who has become a dear friend.

To the American Cancer Society both at the national level and especially our local unit, for their total support.

To Frank Pinchbeck, my neighbor and good friend who graciously made corrections. (passed away 7/97)

To Connie Aquilino, Priscilla Sakal, Andy and Marcy Schwartz for their help with corrections.

To Michael Korda, who answered many questions about this book and for his support.

—Dennis O'Hara

I also thank the men in our support group, especially those who were interviewed, my co-author and good friend Dennis O'Hara, my wife Sandra and children, Marcy, Andy and his wife Robin, Barrie and her husband Jeffrey for their unwavering support. To Jim Mullen who founded Man to Man in 1990. Jim passed away January 16, 1997. Even during these last few years when Jim was in failing health, he continued to be helpful to others. He was always willing to give advice and he spoke to our own Dennis many times. We dedicate this book to Jim's memory.

—Jules Schwartz

Our Founder, Mentor and Friend

James F. Mullen
1918-1997

If I can stop one heart from breaking,
I shall not live in vain;
If I can ease one life the aching, Or cool one pain,
Or help one fainting robin Unto his nest again,
I shall not live in vain.
—Emily Dickinson

INTRODUCTION

Jules Schwartz and I, Dennis O'Hara, have written this book to aid men and their loved ones in the survival of prostate cancer.

After being told I had prostate cancer at age forty nine, I chose a radical prostatectomy which is the surgical removal of the prostate gland. This took place in March of 1992.

I founded the local chapter of Man to Man, a prostate cancer support group in July of 1993, in Dutchess County, NY. I recognized the need for such a group for myself and many others and I will tell you in this book how our support group got started. I will also give you the many pitfalls and insights on starting a support group.

This book will be your service manual so to speak, on prostate cancer. It is written in laymen terms so you can understand and gain much knowledge about prostate cancer without the use of a Medical Dictionary, or having to trek off to your local library.

Since I formed our support group, I have spoken to many, many, men and their families and have counseled some of these men including physicians, attorneys and clergy on this subject.

Jules Schwartz, my co-author, has had and is still receiving many different types of chemotherapy. Some are very experimental and new, since he was diagnosed with stage D prostate cancer (see glossary) in February of 1993. Jules and I have spoken to many health groups and civic clubs, including Rotary, IBM, Elks, etc., about prostate cancer and have become self taught experts on this subject.

In this book you will learn how to achieve long term survival and even learn the difference between <u>PROSTATE</u> cancer and <u>PROSTRATE</u> cancer.

Another important reason for this book is that most books, by doctors or laymen, cover only the beginning "A" and "B" stages (see glossary) of prostate cancer. These books tend to be very technical and really do not tell the average man much about various treatments. Our book does.

However, that is only a small part of the story. A very large number of men are past stages "A" and "B" and must seek treatments other than surgery or radiation. These men may be young or old, but have some medical conditions which makes surgery too risky. They may choose other options instead. We discuss these in the "Support Group" chapter, just as if you would be at one of our meetings and questioning one of the men about their particular choice of treatment such as surgery, radiation, seed implantation, cryosurgery, combined hormonal therapy, neoadjuvant therapy, chemotherapy and yes, even watchful waiting. We even discuss the latest on intermittent hormonal therapy and much more. Also, what is seldom mentioned in other books is that in those who choose surgery, or radiation, nearly half are not successful and there is a recurrence.

There are billions of cancer cells that are invisible. They can escape from the prostate to other places. Unfortunately, this is often not discovered until after the surgery or radiation. It is something that the doctor is not to blame for.

This book goes beyond stages "A" and "B" and that is what makes it different and worthwhile.

Our book is unique, not because of the two different approaches we and our doctors chose to fight PCa, but because we know over 150 men who chose many different options for PCa. We have candid stories from some of these men that we would like to share with you, along with what the support group did and continues to do for them and their families.

There is also a chapter on the Side by Side group for the significant others of PCa survivors. These ladies stand tall with us through the whole ordeal of prostate cancer and deserve a tremendous amount of credit and recognition.

"If you always do what you always did
You always get what you always got"

Quote is from Lovell Jones PHd.
Dr. Jones found this quote on a bathroom wall somewhere in New England. The author is unknown.

Part 1

AUTOBIOGRAPHY of JULES SCWHARTZ

I was born in Poughkeepsie N.Y. 70 years ago. My life has been a happy one. I served in the army during World War II. I then graduated from Baylor University School of business in Waco, Texas. Since then I have been in the advertising business for almost 50 years and am still active.

I was fortunate to marry Sandra over 40 years ago and we have three grown children and seven grandchildren. Sandra has been an invaluable part of my support system. She has a very positive attitude. She attends the meetings of Side by Side which is the sister group to Man to Man. These meetings are headed by the wife of Dennis, Jackie O'Hara. You will read about this in another chapter titled "Side by Side".

Both Sandra and myself have always been interested in community service. Sandra has served as a court monitor, is a hospice volunteer and has volunteered at a local hospital for over 30 years and is still active there. I have been President of The Outdoor Advertising Council of New York, Poughkeepsie South Rotary and Israel Bonds. I'm presently editor of our Man to Man support group bulletin and Vice President to the support group and Dennis' right hand man.

In 1993 I met Dennis O'Hara, the co-author of this book. Although this is my biography, I want to say something about Dennis because he would never say it of himself. He is a most unselfish, giving person. He will talk to a total stranger on the phone for an hour about PCa, a person he may never meet. He gives of his time to lead the Man to Man support group and to talk to various organizations. There is no financial reward. Dennis gets satisfaction knowing that he is helping others.

How my life has changed. I was going along in 1992 like almost everyone else feeling fine and assuming I would never have a serious ailment. That was something that happens to someone else.

During a routine physical, the doctor noticed my prostate was enlarged. This could be a warning sign although almost all men over 50 years old have this and the great majority of these men do not have prostate cancer. There are some warning signs such as frequent night trips to urinate. Prostate cancer like high blood pressure, diabetes or certain heart problems often gives no warning signals. In fact I had none.

I was sent to the urologist who took a PSA (Prostate Specific Antigen) blood test. The count was 17, well over the acceptable "4" number. Therefore a biopsy of the prostate was done.

Finally in February 1993 I got that fateful phone call from the urologist, "I'm sorry Jules, I hate to tell you this, but you have prostate cancer." This was a total shock and I was too upset to talk to him. I put Sandy on the phone and she got all the details from the doctor. The average person knows little if anything about cancer and when you hear the word "cancer" it is very scary to say the least.

There is no way of knowing the exact date, but I have probably had this since about October 1992. We went to a leading urologist at Columbia Presbyterian Hospital in New York City. He mentioned the options of surgery or radiation. (At that time I was 66 and the cut off date for surgery is usually 70). In those days very little information was given out and unfortunately things haven't changed much.

I went in for the surgery. It was never done because they found a "touch" of cancer on one lymph node. It is standard procedure not to operate when this happens.

I was then put on CHT (Combined Hormonal Therapy) treatment. This consisted of Eulexin taken daily in pill form and a monthly injection of Lupron. (Now the Lupron injections are done every three months). This kept the PSA down for twenty months. Each individual is different. Most men last an average of two years on the CHT. However, there are also many cases where it lasts for five years or more. Let me preface history with this observation: For most types of cancer the treatment is pretty cut and dry. Prostate Cancer is a huge grey area once one gets past stage B (Organ Confined). Many books have been written, but a big volume could be written on what we don't know. For stage A and B there is surgery, or radiation, seed implant, combined hormonal therapy or watchful waiting. For advanced cases (C and beyond) there are various possible treatments. What works for one man may not work for another. Usually treatment must be tried to see if it works. If it doesn't as author Michael Korda, in his well written book "Man to Man" recommends, you can find out which doctor has performed the most surgery and what his success record is. He also emphasizes that a second opinion is always important. Advanced cases should also get a second opinion and find an oncologist who has lots of experience with PCa. If you live in a small town, you probably need to travel to a bigger city.

Back to my case, after refracting (becoming resistant to the Hormonal Therapy) we went to a leading Oncologist at Columbia Presbyterian. He recommended Chemotherapy; this was unusual because most men who go on Chemo have had surgery or radiation and I didn't have either. (This again brings out how every case is unique).

Finally in the summer of 1995 I was put on a common chemotherapy treatment consisting of Emcyt which is chemo even though taken orally in pill form (6 pills daily) plus a weekly session of intravenous Velban.

After a few months of this treatment the PSA had gone from 16 to 12. The local oncologist felt 12 was too high and I was taken off this treatment. The treatment was very mild and there were no aftereffects at all.

A year later my present Doctor, (Howard Scher) who is affiliated with Memorial Sloan Kettering, gave the opinion that I had done well and even though my PSA count was 12, it had not only "stabilized" but went down a little. It seems like the oncologist with little experience may be putting too much emphasis on the number whereas the big doctors feel it's more important whether PSA is going up or down and that is the real significance of the number. Here is an example: Let's say a man has a PSA of .7. For someone like myself this would be excellent if that number held. On the other hand someone who just had surgery would be in trouble, because with a .7 a recurrence is indicated. If you have had a radical prostatectomy your PSA should be very close to 0.

After the Chemo treatments a doctor at Columbia Presbyterian put me back on CHT. He is not to be faulted because in some cases a person who has refracted does alright when he is put back on this treatment at a later date. There is no way of knowing unless you try. As mentioned before everyone is different. In my case this did not work and the PSA kept going up. I was then put on another chemo regimen consisting mainly of Cyclophosphomate (a powerful chemical administered intravenously used almost exclusively to combat small cell type of lung cancer) and this did not work either.

Finally Dr. Scher put me on Taxol. Another chapter explains exactly what this is. This is a powerful treatment. Although the amount administered is not a lot, it takes 3 hours of intravenous because it enters the body just one drop at a time. (Recently there was an article in a medical journal that scientists are trying to come up with a way to convert the Taxol to pills or some other way where intravenous will no longer be necessary). So far, so good; I am about to receive the last of 6 treatments. The PSA "stabilized" at 55. Then it went down ten points. When this treatment is completed I will have to be watched, with hopes that it will last a long time.

I would like to close by commenting on 3 things: My physical condition, my mental condition and our Man to Man support group.

Physically: Although I have had PCa for 5 years or close to it, I have almost always felt good. The only exception was a minor sore on my gum in my mouth which developed after the 5th Taxol treatment. This is a very common reaction. It lasted for 5 days. It was annoying during the day and sometimes became painful at night. The only other physical change is a substantial loss of hair although I'm lucky to still have a pretty good amount. I have never missed a day of work and we travel to Israel to see our family there twice a year. We also go to Vermont often because we like it there.

Mentally: My whole life has been affected, a lot in a positive way. You become aware of your own mortality and you therefore try to make every day count. No matter how well a person is doing, he must realize this is a disease that could be potentially fatal. I think a good word to describe this feeling is "scary."   I never lost any friends over this as some people have. As a matter of fact I have met many beautiful people including Dennis O'Hara in our support group who I otherwise would have never met. I have never been depressed. The secret here is to keep busy and not to allow this disease to rule your life.

An observation: Some books on PCa claim that a man's first concern when he learns he has PCa are the two "I"s — Impotency and Incontinence. This may be true in some cases especially if the man is in his 40's or 50's. In my case and I think in most cases when you learn you have PCa your first thought is to stay alive as long as possible. That is still my thinking today. I have had a great life for 70 years, with a great family, naturally I will try to stay around as long as possible.

In another chapter it is mentioned that 200 possible cancer cures are being researched. I guess if one stays around long enough, one of these might work out.

Last but not least: Our local Man to Man support group. Credit goes to Dennis for starting this and the American Cancer Society deserves thanks for sponsoring us. I have always been in this group and I am his right-hand man. He describes in the chapter on "Support Group" why this is so important. We are upbeat. We are informative. Also, we can boost morale. I never could under-stand how anyone with PCa would not attend these meetings con-sidering all the benefits.

It is now January 1997. About 6 months have passed since the above. A new appointment was made with Dr. Scher for January 8th-back in July. No further treatment was prescribed. I had just finished the Taxol and this was at least partly successful. The PSA has gone down from 55 to 35. Late last September, I carried some heavy baggage on a trip to Baltimore and then had back pain. We went to an orthopedist. He took X-rays and said the back was sprained. This seemed logical at the time. Physical Therapy was prescribed but did not help.

We then went to a neurologist who also specializes in backs. He sent me for an MRI that same day. This showed one of my hot spots of the lower spine had become a tumor. This was the prob-lem and the reason for all the pain. The very next day I went for the first of 13 radiation treatments. The tumor was "zapped out" and the discomfort has gone.

Meanwhile in early December I got a shot of Lupron that lasts one month to hold me over until the next doctors visit. Finally came the January 8th appointment. Although I had blood work done at a local lab including a PSA, the doctor did not have these results because the lab forgot to fax them.

Dr. Scher does not worry a lot about the PSA if the patient is feeling good, which I am. In December we went to Israel. I still go to work every day and next week we go back to Vermont.

For the time being I'm on Zoladex (like Lupron, but lasts 3 months instead of one). If the PSA keeps going up, it's possible I could be put on Taxol again. It would be alright if my PSA is a high number as long as it stabilizes.

There are always new developments. The doctor must decide which treatment has the best chance of success in each particular case.

You have to be happy to be feeling well, make the most of each day and not let the PCa rule your life. This is exactly what I am doing.

It is now October 1997. I am still on Zoladex. My PSA has risen to 130, so I asked Dr. Scher why he keeps me on this. He said if he didn't my PSA would even be worse. I recently had a CT and Bone scan. The CT was good, showing no spread of cancer from the bone where it has been for 2 years. However the Bone scan showed more hot spots plus a small tumor on my right hip.

In this situation I will deal with a local radiation-oncology group. They in turn consult with Dr. Scher. There are 2 possible treatments and I am having both. Already an injection of Strontium 89 has been administered. This treatment consists of radioactive fluid that goes thru my entire system. It increases calcium in the bones. You are less likely to get any more lesions and it also helps with pain and lowers the PSA.

The other treatment is external beam radiation. It will treat the localized area where the tumor is. It consists of about 12 five - minute treatments and I will begin them around Oct. 14,1997.

Future outlook: Above treatments could be given again in the future. Object is to stay at D2 stage, or not to have cancer advance beyond the bone. We are buying time hoping they come up with more effective treatments in the future.

"Knowledge without wisdom results in foolishness"

From the book of Proverbs.

Chapter 1

AUTOBIOGRAPHY of DENNIS O'HARA
THE PROVERBIAL "I felt a lump"—August'91

Shocking title, but that is how it all started for me. The digital
rectal exam (DRE) had produced a lump. The doctor said not to
worry and in my eyes, whenever they say that, it's a clue to worry.
My next step was the famous PSA (Prostate Specific Antigen). I
thought initially that it had something to do with U.S.A. and this
test would confirm my citizenship! I immediately went from my
doctor's office to the hospital with the prescription in hand and
lubricating jelly all over and I got the PSA test.

I must say that at age 49, I was not all too concerned with
prostate cancer. The urologist that I was going to for 26 years, was
unaware of the protocol for the PSA test, which I would unfortunately come to realize. I did find out the protocol is as such; first,
the PSA should be done, then the DRE. This order is required
because it seems that a false reading can be reached by performing the DRE first, since the exam itself stimulates the prostate to
put out more PSA.

The test was completed and I went home to my dear wife
Jackie with the news of "the lump." We laughed it off, (so to
speak) and went on with our lives as usual. This was in August of
'91. The report came back at a level of 1.9 and the doctor said
that was good news. I felt that there was something wrong. My
body was telling me that something was up. Ejaculation was burning at times and I was often not looking forward to sex. I did have
prior problems, prostatitis to be exact. Sitz baths and antibiotics
cured that problem, but at age 49, this was a different experience
entirely. The urologist told me to see him in 4 to 6 months and we
would take it from there. I spoke to my brother Frank who is 8
years my junior. He had talked to his doctor who confirmed the
proper protocol for the PSA.

My wife and I decided to seek the advice of a local urologist, recommended to us by my wife's cousin whose husband is a local pediatrician. I made the appointment with this doctor, Dr. Bernard Salevitz, in October of 1991. I assumed the position and the DRE was completed. The tissues to clean the lubricating jelly were dispensed and he left the room. I cleaned myself as best as I could, as I was rushing in fear that someone would enter the room and find me with my pants down and in this awful position, trying to wipe the lubricating jelly off my personal parts and legs.

Dr. Salevitz finally came back and confirmed the existence of this lump. He advised me that I should repeat the PSA test after a two week waiting period, because the prostate gland was now stimulated and false negatives can be achieved. So after the waiting period, I had a repeat PSA. It was also below a 4 (about a 1.9) I felt this was good news.

Dr. Salevitz saw me 3 weeks after the second PSA and did another "assume the position" digital rectal exam. He confirmed that I should have a biopsy just to rule out problems, in particular, cancer, which at that time was not a word in my vocabulary.

December, 1991, the biopsy was performed at his office and it was quite unforgettable. My legs were on stirrups and the nurse and doctor were there with all sorts of instruments being placed in my rectum. I tried to make light of what was happening to me by relating to how my wife always felt about seeing her gynecologist.

The biopsy was very uncomfortable and I felt snapping feelings as the samples were taken from my prostate, (six in all). It did hurt, but I must say the clean up was the worst. I had to walk to the bathroom with blood running down my legs and clean myself. I felt this was archaic and thought the biopsy should have been done in the hospital.

I did watch it on the monitor as the ultra sound guided procedure was done but I could not tell what end was what. Several days went by and we all felt everything was OK. At 9:00 am, Dr. Salevitz' nurse called and said that the doctor wanted to see me at 10:00 am. We knew then that the "proverbial lump" was a problem. No doctor ever calls and asks to see you unless it's bad news.

Jackie and I drove to the doctor's office full of anxiety and all kinds of thoughts were racing through our heads.

The nurse brought us into the doctor's office where he was already seated reading various reports. He promptly stated that I had prostate cancer, patted me on the shoulder and that was the extent of the information offered. My wife and I were paralyzed with fear and had so many questions to ask and the doctor was ready to dismiss us. We had no knowledge of prostate cancer but we did fear cancer. We thought it was my death sentence and started asking the doctor what it meant. He told us many other tests had to be done to see if the cancer had metastasized, (spread to other body parts); my god, we didn't even know what the word metastasized meant. He said, "See the receptionist Chris," (who, by the way, is a very understanding and caring person and an asset to the Dr.'s office), "and she will set you up with appointments at the hospital and see me in two weeks." That was it. The appointments were made and we left.

As I drove home, I told my wife that I was just handed my death sentence and did not know how to handle it. We both thought it was time to go shopping for a coffin. We arrived home and I went outside on our deck and cried. At suppertime, we announced to our children, Denise, Jackie and Brian, that Dad had prostate cancer. We all cried and I asked them all to be strong, because I needed their strength to get me through this. (There was no support group then, I wish there was. My life and the lives of my family would have been a lot easier at that point in time, if the information the group has now, could have been available to us then).

The next person I called was my chiropractor, Dr. Robert Strange, because I knew he had a background in radiology. He told me to come right over, with my wife and for 45 minutes he explained to us prostate cancer and its many pitfalls. He was and still is a fine chiropractor and man. He spends time with me still and supports my continuous struggle with PCa.

I called my brother Frank and he came the next day. We hugged and cried and he was just as upset and concerned as I was, having lived through a breast cancer ordeal with his wife's mother.

Emma was her name and she had fought the battle with breast cancer for 18 years before losing the war. Emma, or Mimi, as the family called her, would become one of my many inspirations in the battle against prostate cancer.

Frank and I discussed many things that day including death, pain, suffering and most of all living. He made things easier for me as one of my biggest fears was what would happen to my family if I died? Frank assured me he would watch over them and assured me that I was not going to die. He was right, but it was good to know that he would be there for my family.

My mother-in-law, Connie, also came to visit that day. Connie and I have a great relationship that has lasted over 35 years; we were friends before I married her daughter and are still friends now. I admire her strength and opinions and she too is one of my inspirations. Connie assured me, between tears, that all would be OK, and just in case it wasn't, she too would be there for me and the family. These things are important to cancer patients since we are concerned about our families, in the event we cross over. Knowing someone will help look out for your family makes the diagnosis of cancer easier to digest.

My wife Jackie was also strong for me and promised to take care of me no matter what shape or form the cancer turned out to be. So knowing Frank, Connie and Jackie, besides my children, were taking this in stride and all handling it, I decided to move on and stop feeling sorry for myself.

My parents, Ray and Sue and most of the rest of my family lived in Florida, their long distance support and prayers were with me.

I tried to find out about prostate cancer from people I knew who had it. My friend Bill had it 10 years prior to my diagnosis, but he had died from a ruptured aorta. I phoned Bill's wife Mary, who is a nurse and picked her brain for an hour. Mary is also a very close friend and I regarded her personal and professional opinion high on my list. Mary told me about Bill's PCa and how he remained clean for over eight years after his radical and that if I was to have cancer, this was the best kind. At the time I thought this strange because I didn't want any cancer, even a good kind.

My dad, 84 at the time, was pretty healthy and active with no prostate problems. Both my brother Ray, in his late 50's and my brother Frank, early 40's, had no prostate problems. My sisters, Sue and Eileen, along with my mother, were also cancer free. So with that, I felt that prostate cancer was out of the picture for me. That proved not to be the case.

In any event, the Bone scan, CAT scan, X-rays and blood tests all showed no spread of the disease.

As you will see later on in the book, the support group provides much more information and support for newly diagnosed men then I ever dreamed of.

About one year before my diagnosis, Mary had given me a Bible that had belonged to Bill. Now, I must tell you that God played and still plays a big part in my survival and my life.

This is where the term PROSTRATE and PROSTATE comes into play. I feel I coined this phrase, as I always tell people at the group meeting or while I am doing a talk in front of health concerned people that PROSTRATE is the position you assume after you get the news from the doctor that you have PROSTATE CANCER, you get on your hands and knees and assume the PROSTRATE position and ask God, "Why me?"

While sitting in the X-ray room, I had brought Bill's Bible to read during my wait. Since all three tests, the Bone scan, the CAT scan and the chest X-ray were scheduled for the same day, it would take hours to complete them. My wife was waiting patiently upstairs in the Test Connection area at St. Francis Hospital, which is quite unique as it is a very comfortable staging area to wait in, with music, reading materials, bathrooms, etc.

In the X-ray area there were many people waiting, one was a Priest and another male stranger who was sitting next to me on my left. As I was reading The Bible, the stranger on my left asked me what I was reading. I told him it was a best seller, The Bible. The priest immediately perked up and the man next to me said "why don't you turn to Psalm 91."

I must tell you that my friend Bill had died 2 years before my diagnosis, in his Bible there was nothing underlined so far from what I had read and I had already read up to Psalm 89. Well I did as the stranger requested and I turned to Psalm 91. Lo and behold underlined was a message from Bill, the first few verses and many of the rest telling me that all is well and God will defend and protect me. The stranger started praying over me and placed his hands on my shoulder and head, the Priest got up and left and I was speechless. The stranger assured me all would be OK. Everyone in the waiting room was astounded at this gentleman praying over me.

The technician came in and told me I could leave, all the X-rays were completed and I should return in 3 hours to finish the Bone scan. I rushed upstairs to tell Jackie about Bill's message and the stranger and realized that I did not thank this man. There was only one way in and out of the X-ray area and as I returned to thank him, he was nowhere to be found. I must tell you that this is not a fiction story, it really happened to me and I tell this story often to anyone who will listen.

As I returned upstairs to the Test Connection area, I told Jackie that all would be fine and showed her Psalm 91 that was under-lined in Bill's Bible. **(see page 219)** She was astounded to say the least and several days later we got the good news that all the tests were negative for the spread of the cancer.

In January of 1992, I met with the doctor to discuss my options. He talked about surgery, radiation, or doing nothing. I was 50 then, so doing nothing was out of the question, the doctor did not like the idea of radiation in my case because he felt in 10 years the cancer might return. He felt that I was a very good candidate for surgery, which removes the prostate and the cancer.

Believe me, my wife and I were like two fish out of water here and we did not know what to do. There was no one to get advice from or to speak to about prostate cancer. All this has changed, I have formed the local chapter of Man to Man, a prostate cancer support group here in Dutchess County, N.Y.

The doctor suggested that I see an oncologist (another new word for us). We didn't even know what kind of doctor that was. We thought that seeing this doctor was our last chance for sur-vival since he was a cancer doctor.

As it turned out we saw a local Oncologist, Dr. Glenn Agoliati, who spoke to us for about an hour and answered our questions and concerns and told me that in my case surgery would work very well. He was and still is, a very caring doctor. All the emo-tions and fears that we felt have been discussed in many other books and I agree with them all, so I won't be repetitive in this area.

"Knowledge equals Survival"

"If you falter in times of trouble how weak is your strength"

From the Book of Proverbs

Chapter 2

THE RADICAL PROSTATECTOMY (surgery)

 T he doctor suggested that I give my own blood for the surgery
that I was about to endure. I was to give one pint per week. This
was fine with me as I wanted to be cured of cancer and not possibly come home with some other problem from possible blood
contamination. He also set the date for the surgery, March 16,
1992. This was very significant to me since it was one day before
St. Patrick's day. This was a good sign, since I am part Irish.
Waiting for the surgery was the pits. It turned out to be very
stressful, with fears that the cancer would spread during the wait.

The sex question did not really become a part of our lives,
because I always felt as a man, I did not have to prove myself in
the bedroom. There are many other things in life besides sex, and
after talking with hundreds of men in person and hundreds of
hours on the phone with men regarding this prior treatment question about sex, it proved to be very insignificant where survival
seems to be the first concern. In my case the doctor felt because
of my age and my general health all my functions would return to
normal after the surgery and he was right.

The blood was given 4 weeks prior to surgery, one pint per
week. It was no big deal for me, but after the 4th pint I did get
real tired and dizzy. I highly suggest giving your own blood if possible. It's a great feeling that your own blood will be going back
inside you and not a stranger's. That is one less stressful element
that you will have to battle.

The big day arrived, for the surgery; my wife Jackie and my
daughter Jackie, took the ride to the hospital with me at 5:30 am.
We had no idea what to expect. Fortunately, today things are different and anyone who is diagnosed with cancer should seek out
a support group prior to any form of cancer treatment. They really are our first line of defense in this battle against cancer, (more
on that later).

We chose St. Francis Hospital, (I say we because you must include your family, spouse, children etc. in making this kind of decision) because it has religious statues on every floor, Catholic Nuns all over the place and a Catholic Priest for the chaplain. I needed all the help I could get here on earth and from up above. It proved a good choice. Checking in was very uneventful, blood samples were taken to make sure I was really me and the blood I gave matched my body, I said good-by to the two Jackies in my life and I was whisked away to the holding area. I was then told to disrobe and put on one of those stupid hospital gowns and a hat. An IV was administered and I immediately mellowed out. A very nice man shaved and prepped me for the operation and we discussed our cats. I have three of them.

Once more I saw my two Jackies and into the operating room I went before you could say prostate. Everyone was dressed in green and masked. I could not see my Doctor and I remember wondering if they knew why I was there. The O.R. nurse stroked my forehead and asked how I was doing, I said fine. She then asked me why I was here and I responded, "they say I have prostate cancer." This was a good question and answer because I did not want a leg or an arm or my testicles removed by mistake.

The anesthesiologist came over and asked my name, I told him Dennis but everyone I know calls me IGGY. Well he said "good night IGGY," and the next thing I knew I was with a nurse, waking me up in the recovery room.

At the time I did not feel any pain. All I was thinking was had the surgery progressed to the removal of the prostate. The doctor had told me the first thing they do during the surgery is to remove the lymph nodes and have a pathologist test them for the spread of cancer. If it is in the lymph system the surgery is discontinued because the horse is already out of the barn so to speak and to continue the surgery is useless. After the prostate is removed another pathology test is done to see if the cancer has reached the margins of the prostate or broken through it. If it has, this is not great news.

As I was drifting in and out, in the recovery room, these thoughts were on my mind. I noticed one of the recovery room nurses did not look too happy, I asked her what was up. She told me that she was having a bad day; imagine that if she was having a bad day what the heck would my day be considered.

I always look at things with a degree of humor. You must have a sense of humor, or you will wallow away in self pity and that really stinks. I asked the nurse why her day was not going so well; "marital problems" was her answer. I can't remember what we discussed, but it was my first counseling job as a cancer survivor and later on my counseling efforts would continue with great success regarding cancer, that is. Whatever I said perked her up and she held my hand and we exchanged eye contact with each other and I knew she felt better. She must have seen the concern in my eyes about the pathology reports, because she got my chart and held my hand again and quietly whispered "pathology reports are negative." Hallelujah, thank God and I fell back to sleep.

Later on I was to find out that the surgeon had sent out a Catholic nun during the operation and informed my family that all was well the lymph nodes looked clear and the operation would continue. When it was over Dr. Salevitz spoke to them to inform all present that the surgery had gone well and that I was going to be fine. This was something that the doctor didn't have to do but he did. I think that when surgeons keep the family apprised of the ongoing operation, it is a credit to them.

Several hours later, I awoke in my room with my wife (Jackie#1) and the rest of my family at my bedside. Also with me were a combination of tubes, hoses, pipes and machines hooked up everywhere. One IV was for nutrition, another for medication, there were also some crazy looking things wrapped around my legs inflating and deflating every minute or so. This I later found out was to prevent blood clots. There was a catheter (a tube inserted in my penis) so urine would flow into a bag hanging on the side of my bed, another tube coming out of my stomach, to drain the blood and other liquid out of the area where my prostate used to be; man was I scared! Really scared!

I had been hospitalized several times in my life, once for a compound fracture of my right femur, (I spent four months in the hospital) so I knew how to adapt quite well to hospital rules etc. This was something else; here I was stapled from stem to stern (belly button down to my penis) and all wrapped up including a catheter and a groin drain.

My family all smiled and said, "Hi dad you did great; it's all over and you're OK. " Little did they know that I already knew about the negative pathology reports from my new found friend in the recovery room.

Morphine couldn't be used to ease the pain since I was allergic to it. This really was a bummer for me. The pain began to set in now and everything they tried for the next 4 days didn't help. Even my wife was mad at me. I physically hurt so bad I was really mean to her and even asked her to leave. She used to bring her knitting along with her and sit there all day and into the night and watch me and help me eat, etc. Jackie made it a lot easier for me and it really was mean of me to tell her to get out, but it was the pain talking not me. I apologized a few days later.

My friends and family called and some visited. The days were fair but the nights were miserable because of the pain. Second to the pain my main concern was when would I be allowed to get out of bed? I have 2 herniated discs and staying in bed or lying on my back for too long causes severe leg pain or sciatica. Well it was 4 days before I could get out of bed.

Every day Dr. Salevitz or one of his associates would come in and assure me that all was fine with the recovery process from the surgery and that they were trying everything for the pain. The little ball shaped device hanging from my stomach was filling up with blood each day and after it cleared up (about 4 days) the doctor said he was going to remove it. I asked him if it was going to hurt and his reply was "YES," and that I might want to take a deep breath because there really was not an easy way to remove it. Well he was right! It hurt like heck and I felt like my stomach was being torn out.

Now don't forget, that was over 5 years ago. Today things are different. There are more drugs for pain, shorter hospital stays, shorter surgical procedures and less blood loss during surgery. This makes it an easier procedure; some men have it done in less then two hours and use only 1 pint of blood and are out of bed the next day, home in 5 days. My operation took over 4 hours with three pints of my own blood used, four days in bed and home in 7 days. This is not a bad reflection on my surgery, things have improved today.

The support group, if it were in existence then as it is today, would have eased almost all of my fears and frustrations and streamlined everything.

The food was great and my care givers were out of this world. They treated me like a V.I.P., tending to my every need. Starting a support group had not even entered my mind yet. I was not a famous politician, attorney, doctor, author, or actor. Any notoriety could not precede my stay at St. Francis Hospital. As an ordinary guy, I was treated great.

As I said before, this book is to inform you about our support group, so I won't go into medical terminology or my daily hospital routine.

The 7 days went by slowly and during that time all was explained to me about my pains, aches and the catheter. One night about 2 am, I was awakened by the nurse on duty. She asked me about my surgery as her husband had just been diagnosed with PCa. She wanted to know how I felt and if my sex life would resume and many other things. I could not answer about the sex part yet, so we discussed in great detail how I felt, (my second counseling session). This seemed very strange to me; here I was in a surgical ward and a surgical nurse was asking me about my condition. At that time, a seed was planted in my mind to learn more about prostate cancer, to share my findings and experience with other men in order to make their journey with the disease a lot easier.

The day of discharge had finally arrived, March 23, 1992. No big fanfare here; the doctor came in and removed some of the staples from the incision and told me that I had been through a war zone and I was doing good. He asked me to see him in 1 week to remove the remaining staples. The duty nurse explained how to clean the catheter and put on the leg bag that was to collect the urine. As far as transportation, no trains, buses, or planes, just me and my wife and an old Subaru wagon. On the way home we stopped at the local pharmacy to pick up antibiotics and then home, about a 25 minute drive from the hospital.

*"Apply your heart to
instruction and your
ears to words of knowledge"*

From the Book of Proverbs.

CHAPTER 3

THE HEALING PROCESS

T hings were quite different now, a catheter was my constant companion at home for the next 21 days.

I did not have to worry about returning to work because I had retired several years earlier from the construction field with back problems.

We have a split level home and 3 bathrooms, so I was able to get comfortable on every level of my home. The pain was bearable now and I was just taking Tylenol occasionally and Cipro an antibiotic for prevention of any infections that might occur.

I would learn later on that many men have worse post surgical problems then I ever imagined could exist. I was very lucky in this sense. The surgery went smooth and the healing process moved along quite well. Doctor Salevitz had done a fine job.

The catheter in my penis was the pits; it was constantly pulling and tugging and urine leaked out of my penis when I sat down or had a bowel movement. I could not imagine why they did not have a check valve in the large urine bag to stop back flow, as this always happened when I sat down and got up. Several times as I took a shower the top of the bag got drenched and it was a real nuisance to hold the bag as I showered. As you all know, necessity is the mother of all inventions. One day I just disconnected the big urine bag and showered without it. The urine just ran down my leg into the shower drain. This was a big improvement while I showered and I recommend it.

The leg bag enabled me to get out and around, but was strapped to my thigh and presented problems, so one day I sent my wife to the local drug store where she purchased another leg bag. I then got some plastic tubing from my son's aquarium. I extended the tubing from my Foley catheter (the tube in my penis) to the leg bag which I now put on my ankle; this works great and it has a check valve. The small bag fills up quite quickly so this ankle extension hook up made it very easy to empty. All you had to do was to put your leg on the toilet bowl, pull the plug and let it empty. You don't even have to shake it!

I got stronger every day, but was very anxious about getting this tube out of my penis.

My first trip to the doctor's office was about 7 days after I got home from the hospital. He removed the rest of the staples and I insisted on the removal of the penal tube. He was very adamant about this and boldly told me no way! Later on I was to learn this was a wise decision on his part, as the tube (catheter) is not only there to allow urine to flow through the urethra, but it prevents scar tissue from forming. The urethra is severed during the surgery and if scar tissue forms and it gets closed, there are big problems with urine backup. Most likely you would have to be catheterized (opening of the urethra using a plastic tube allowing urine to flow freely).

The doctor told me prior to surgery about the possibility of incontinence (urinating yourself) and impotence (erection problems) after surgery, but as I look back on that conversation it was just a blur and it did not really sink in at the time.

Jackie and I had made the decision for the surgery without consulting anyone or any books. We did not do any research at all.

You must remember the support group was not here yet. I still would have chosen the surgery but with some other fringe benefits attached. One being the combined hormonal therapy. I would have taken it for at least 3 months prior to surgery had I known about this. This procedure would have possibly improved my odds greatly in keeping the cancer contained to the prostate.

Back to the healing process now. After about twenty-eight days of the penis tube the big day arrived. I thought the doctor was going to remove it but to my surprise the nurse did it.

Jackie had gone out and bought a large assortment of some "wee wee" pads as we called them and some pads for our bed in anticipation for the "Big Whiz" leakage after the catheter was removed. It didn't happen. No "Big Whiz" from the first day that the nurse with her expertise removed it with no fuss, no pain. She just deflated the little balloon inside; how I don't know and I don't care. She told me to take a deep breath and that was it, the penis tube gone forever. The nurse told me to call her at 10:00AM and 4:00PM to see how my flow was. If there was any blood in my urine, if I had any control of stopping and starting the flow of urine.

The drive home from the doctors office was about twenty-five minutes and I felt like I was a new man without the hoses and bag attached to me. As soon as we arrived home I had to urinate.

I was and am still very lucky with no urination problems from day one.

My flow was good and control was OK. I credit this to my constantly doing the Kegel exercises or pelvic muscle floor training exercises. I have always had a nervous twitch if I can call it that. I constantly squeezed and still do, the cheeks of my butt together, even years before my surgery. I guess this is one case where a nervous habit paid off.

At 12:00 I called the nurse and told her I had a good flow of urine, good control starting and stopping and no blood. She said this was good. At 4:00 PM I repeated the same information to her. The nurse also told me if anything changed to call the office and let her know. This was on a Friday so here I was, to face my "Whiz a roo" fate all weekend alone with the doctors office closed. All went well and we didn't need the pads on the bed, but I slept with them anyway for about 10 days. As far as wetting my pants I did have a few times where I had accidents but I figured that women go through this too, especially in their golden years due to child bearing. If they can do it so can I. I know a lot of men wet themselves and feel very embarrassed and have to wear diapers, but it is better then being dead. I know plenty of men in our support group who are incontinent and have learned to either control it or live with it. Their stories will follow mine when we reach the chapter on support group.

I did wear some diaper pads for about 2 weeks. I used to cut them in half and make a cup for my penis just to catch the little squirts I had from yelling or laughing or getting up or sitting down too fast.

The healing process took a long time even though I did not have to work. I was quite active before the surgery, as active as someone with back problems can be. I liked to walk and each day

I walked in the house till I got tired or my back hurt. I was still hurting somewhat, a deep hurt aching in my rectum and groin area, but not enough to keep me down.

In May I saw Doctor Salevitz and he told me my recovery was progressing very well I was now at the point where most men were 4 to 6 months after surgery, I was only 2 months out of surgery.

He asked me about my erections and I felt quite taken back to tell him about it, there were not any yet. He told me that it would take some time. It did, about sixteen months. I don't want to discuss our sex life because what my wife and I have in the bedroom is sacred and I will not betray my wife's trust and go into it. I can tell you that it did rise to the occasion and fought a semi rigid battle. Finally with a lot of patience from my wife the war was won.

The doctor told me I would need a PSA blood test every 4 to 6 months, a Bone scan and chest X-ray yearly. I would be followed very closely for 2 years and after that not so closely for 3 more years.

Never did I realize the PSA blood test would become as important to me as toilet paper is to America. My first PSA following the surgery was done in June, 1992 and the results were less then 0.1. The doctor and I were overjoyed at this and I thanked God a lot that day.

Life was getting back to normal, but the thought of cancer was still there daily and overwhelming at times. My family was there for me always but there were so many questions that needed to be answered and my emotions were running wild.

One strange thing about the diagnosis of cancer. We actually lost some of our friends, possibly because of their fear that they might catch cancer from me or the fear that I might die.

So months rolled by and the physical recuperation was going well, but the mental and emotional part was way down. Through the winter of 1992, and into 1993, my thoughts were still running wild and my fears of dying from prostate cancer were starting to consume my days and nights. I was funneling my energies into the "why me?" syndrome.

One day I was reading the local newspaper and I saw a small article in it about The American Cancer Society having a meeting for a group of people who have had various forms of cancer. It is called the The Patients Support Group. The meetings were held at 4:30; a weird hour I thought, and it would disrupt supper time in our house, so I put off going. Something was gnawing at my insides and I needed to talk to someone about prostate cancer and many other cancer related issues concerning my fears.

*"It is not good to have zeal
without knowledge
Nor to be hasty and miss the
way"*

Proverbs 19

Chapter 4

SUPPORT GROUP

Finally, in March of 1992, I attended a meeting at the American Cancer Society in Poughkeepsie N.Y. called The Patients Support Group.

Most of the people there were women, about a dozen in all and much to my surprise, there were two men besides me, they also had prostate cancer. "Wow" I thought; I am not the only one in the world with this disease. LB was one of these men and he would later become a very close friend to me and my family. He was 76 at the time. Anyway, the group was not fulfilling my needs. The women would discuss breast and cervical cancers, they weren't going to show me their cervix or breast. I was not going to show them where the scar from my surgery was either. There were some lung cancers there and I could sense the compassion that these ladies had for each other and how positive some of them were about their cancers and their treatments, etc.

There was a lot of crying and emotions were running high because one of the ladies in the group was at home and terminal with breast cancer. These ladies were good for each other, but I really could not relate to them about my erections and my little urination accidents I was having, after all they were women.

Back to the drawing board. Should I put an add in the paper for other men to meet at my home to discuss prostate cancer? I knew LB and the other man FA, would come.

My wife thought I was crazy and that I should just ask my doctor about the things that were bothering me. Little did she know that most doctors don't spend time talking to their patients; it's not their fault they are just too busy. There are a lot of sick people in this world and while most doctors listen to us patients, they just don't hear us.

I did and still do read certain Bible scriptures daily. A message jumped out to me that my friend Bill had underlined. It very subtlety told me not to give up, keep searching and I will find an answer. With this and many other scriptures in my mind, I decided to start my own prostate cancer support group.

In April of 1993 I called the local office of the American Cancer Society and spoke to Cathy Close (more on her later); I explained my plans to her. She did not think there were any other prostate support groups in Dutchess County. She thought it was a good idea but she would have to check with division headquarters and get back to me. Bureaucratic red tape took over at the division level of the ACS and they really dragged their feet.

Locally the ACS liked my idea, since no other group existed in Dutchess County or any other surrounding counties. The closest one was in New York City at Memorial Sloan Kettering Cancer Center.

During the next few months, numerous phone conversations between Cathy Close and I took place. She was trying her best to get the division section of the American Cancer Society to approve my request to start a support group for prostate cancer survivors. The ACS division wanted to know what sort of expertise I held in being a facilitator. Facilitator was a new word for me. "Wow" I thought to myself. What a title I would have if this group was okayed by the ACS.

After all, my only credentials were my past and present experience with prostate cancer. My deep gut feeling was that something had to be done for the countless number of men and their families who didn't know beans about prostate cancer. I really wanted to give back something because I felt lucky to have had a successful outcome from the surgery.

"Had I ever started a group before?" they asked. I answered, "Yes as a matter of fact the group I started was very successful; it consisted of my 3 children and that group is doing just great." This answer did not go over too well with the ACS, but as I said before, I always interject humor into everything I do and if one doesn't laugh life will be pretty dull.

Well, the top guns of the ACS finally conceded, they would agree to my request for a support group, but first I had to go to Syracuse N.Y. and spend a day learning how to be a facilitator. Jackie decided to go along for the ride and she also sat in on my learning session. We both graduated facilitator school with flying colors.

By the way, the school consisted of a day learning how to talk to people who have cancer and learning how to ask the right questions. It also assured the ACS that we were not going to step on any ones toes, or make any one feel bad. We also learned about the ground rules which must be adhered to at support group meetings, especially if you are going to be affiliated with the ACS.

Things began to really move along at this point, my dream of starting a support group was becoming a reality now. A huge amount of support from the ACS at all levels started to take place. The local news Media was notified and our first meeting was held on July 15, 1993.

Ironically it was held in the same room as The Patients Support Group was held and the room could hold only about 8 to 10 people max. Cathy and I felt this room was big enough for Man to Man, the name picked for our group. A man from Florida named Jim Mullens started the first Man to Man prostate cancer support group. Jim and the ACS finally got together and the ACS has adopted the Man to Man concept into their programs.

The room was not big enough for our first meeting, there were seventeen men that night and they spilled out into the hallway. I must say, I was scared to death, since all of the negative things that my family and friends had said about starting a group for prostate cancer survivors started to race through my mind and I did not know where to begin. I had asked for this and now it was here and big mouth me was stumped. I really wanted to run away and hide.

Everyone became real quiet and all eyes turned to me. I looked around the room very slowly, sweating and my blood pressure was probably sky high. The men were waiting for something to happen, little did they know, so was I.

Finally I said "Good evening, I am Dennis O'Hara, a prostate cancer survivor, would you all kindly sign the attendance sheet that I pass around."

Those magical words prostate cancer survivor went over real big; some loud cheers and applause followed, we were on our way. The support group was officially formed and I was and still am the FACILITATOR, a fancy name for leader.

Things really started to move on with many, many questions about the support group, etc. I remembered that Cathy had given me an envelope to give to one of the men. His name was Jules Schwartz. I asked if he were present and I gave him the package. This was my first meeting with Jules who has become my second in command. He is a great friend and also co-author of this book.

Jules is a very caring person. He gives of his time and he advertises our support group on his company's billboards throughout Dutchess County. Jules is our recording secretary, so I have to say nice things about him or I will get stuck doing the minutes.

The meeting continued and my next statement was that we were not here to bash the doctors or the medical community, or to give out any medical advice (this is one of the requirements of the ACS so it is very important to open up every meeting with this statement). It is essential because that's not what the support group is about. We are there to support each other in every way we can, the doctors will not hold your hand and kiss you good night, but the support group will, so to speak.

With each passing minute my nervousness subsided and my unknown and untapped leadership qualities started to emerge.

Questions were being fired at me from every angle. Some of them were very impressive and technical. I realized these guys knew a lot, and had a lot to share. Someone asked about survival rates and statistics. My answer went over big here, "I don't believe in statistics, all of us in this room are separate individuals and we all will stay alive as long as we can and the hell with experts and their statistics." Well they all cheered and now I really was their so called "leader." I also feel that prostate cancer is a crap shoot and any choice you make whether it's surgery, radiation, chemo, hormones or any other treatment, it is not cut and dry. The only certain thing about prostate cancer is the support group, Man to Man. We will be here for each other and unlike the doctors and other professionals I am open twenty four hours a day seven days a week and all this is for free.

When you are diagnosed with prostate cancer, your first line of defense is the support group; the men are deeply imbedded in the trenches fighting this battle with cancer on a one to one basis. The more you can learn, the better your chances are to win the war. I remember one of my earliest slogans was "knowledge equals survival," and Michael Korda in his well written book "Man to Man" refers to this slogan as "helping him cope with prostate cancer."

Another slogan I refer to often is that "I feel we are on a sinking ship, but as long as we keep bailing water, (learning) we will stay afloat."

Here I was in a room with seventeen men, all who were in various stages of prostate cancer, unbelievable, because several weeks ago I was concerned with being able to get 7 or 8 men to show up.

My personal reason for starting the support group was my need to share my deep fears and emotions. I didn't want anybody else to have to go through what my wife and I did, not knowing a thing about prostate cancer. I didn't want fame and there was not any monetary thoughts either; I just wanted to give back. One year had passed since my radical prostatectomy. I felt blessed and just wanted and still do, to help others.

Because of PCa I have met and talked to many men. The wonderful feeling of helping them and their families get through it is just overwhelming. The men often ask me, how do you get through the day? My motto is "Worry about the cancer for 10 to 15 minutes a day," then get on with the rest of your day. In the beginning cancer overwhelmed my days and nights. It took a long time for me to grasp this logic of only thinking and worrying about cancer for a little while, and not to let it consume my every moment.

I don't have the money to travel extensively to get away and forget like some other men do, so we just had to learn how to cope. Our support group provides this for free, we don't even have dues. There are no financial obligations here.

Fame followed me even though I did not look for or expect it. I say fame because of the articles the local papers printed and meeting the men in the group at the mall or in church or many other places. They recognize me and are always stopping to chat and talk about the latest developments regarding PCa. In Michael

Korda's book "Man to Man", he said some very nice things about me and our prostate cancer support group. Michael is a member of our group.

So the group was a "hit" so to speak. Many of the men are charter members and still attend quite regularly. Some have lost the "war," but we continue to "fight the battle for them."

We have outgrown all the rooms at the ACS with our meetings averaging thirty five to fifty men, and when we have a speaker, we get well over 100 men in attendance with their wives. We have moved the meetings to St. Francis Hospital also in Poughkeepsie N.Y. Our mailing list at this point is over 150 and growing. They are all fine gentleman, and amazing as it seems, there is no one who is a pain in the butt. No one asks stupid questions and we all get a chance to speak. I do wish a couple of them would get hearing aids. It would make my job a bit easier.

My concept was to share and that is what we do. We share our lives, our emotions and physical problems for two or more hours the first Thursday of the month at 7PM at St. Francis Hospital.

We always have a satisfied audience and no complaints. My theme for the meetings is to keep it upbeat with a lot of information and not morbid. It is not all doom and gloom and we even laugh a lot. Can you imagine 35 to 50 men sitting around and laughing while discussing prostate cancer, incontinence, impotence, insurance company woes, family problems, doctor patient miseries and yes, even death? We can take it all with a grain of salt and still laugh.

At one particular meeting a lot of us were talking about erection problems and sex. Well, I told the men that I had found a way to solve all erection and sex problems and I made such an announcement. The men were very quiet, after all this was serious stuff, erections and sex. How did I come across this information they asked. What was the remedy and cure all for man's worst plight, not being able to perform in the bedroom?

My answer was simple, I informed them that I had just started a new company (they were all on the edges of their seats). Some were even salivating. At last a cure for impotence! I told them that the name of my company was called "1-800-RENT-A-DICK"; complete humorous pandemonium took over the entire room.

Everyone fell out of their seats as they erupted in laughter. The other people in the building must have thought we were crazy, a cancer group laughing hysterically. That just doesn't happen.

I still use that 800 joke number on occasion especially when new men are at a meeting.

Early on the men decided that they didn't want the women in our meetings because of the personal issues discussed, so my wife formed a Side by Side group, for the women and significant others (more on that later).

We also felt that too many guest speakers would take away our closeness, so we limit them to every three months or so.

The support group was not too popular with the medical community at first. Some of the urologists and the oncologists in our area felt threatened just because of our mere existence, and the fact that we were starting to dispense some good medical information. I have no idea why they felt this way.

We are not doctors or surgeons and don't want to be either. Some of our men were even told to stay away from the support group by their doctors because the doctors felt that we were trouble makers and didn't know what we were talking about and that we were not giving out good information. As the group leader, I took this rather personally and did confront several of the doctors and the hospital administrators to try and change their image of the support group. We were no threat to anybody and the title Man to Man a Prostate Cancer support group is exactly what we stand for. We are not trying to cause trouble for the doctors, but to help the doctors by educating the patient and their families about prostate cancer, something most doctors don't have the time or patience to do. So we explain the options plus the side effects, using personal candid one-on-one interviews with individuals who have been there and back.

The patient gets all this information, in addition to handouts we have. We have a librarian whose name is John Osborne. He is our computer whiz. John gives a lot of his personal time and has created our "Newbie" book which we hand out free to every newly diagnosed man that comes to our meetings. This book is loaded with all the latest information and treatments and all the terminology regarding PCa. When he or she is finished reading it, they can go to his doctor armed with this information and can now make a rational decision on what kind of treatment is best for him.

For the men who can't attend on a regular basis, we keep them informed with our newsletter. Jules takes the minutes and summarizes them and sends them to Gordon Wells.

Gordon then treks off to the ACS headquarters and fires up the copy machine, stuffs the envelopes and mails out over a 100 copies of the minutes from the meeting.

Tony Cerrato puts out the signs to direct new people to the area where we meet.

George Krepp makes the phone calls to arrange for our meeting room to be all set up for us and any visual aids we may need.

We all pull together. This is why our support group is so successful.

At first I did all these jobs myself, while Jackie used to help with the mailings. As the support group grew and my phone calls and behind the scenes meetings with the ACS and many other organizations, in addition to the research projects became very demanding, I had to delegate some of these jobs to others. Another reason I did this was to ease my burden from the result of getting Lyme disease (a debilitating condition from a deer tick, which really drains ones energy). These men were gracious enough to volunteer and are doing a great job.

I also got some very negative feedback from some professional and lay people in regards to using the word SURVIVOR. They felt it was very strong and that it has a strong connection to the HOLOCAUST that took place in Europe where millions of Jews and other races were exterminated. I have discussed this with my co-author Jules who is Jewish and even though my last name is O'Hara and I am of Irish decent, my mother is a Hungarian Jew. Both Jules and I lost relatives in Europe through the holocaust.

Cancer is also a holocaust but in a different way. Many, many people suffer terrible consequences with this disease, some with the chemotherapy aftereffects, some with a lot of emotional and physical changes.

I feel the word SURVIVOR is proper to use in this sense. Now to get back to the negative feeling from the medical community. On one particular occasion one of the local urologists was having a Prostate Cancer Awareness Program sponsored by one of the big drug companies. It was being held at a local restaurant and the newspaper ad gave a number to call to register. It was open to the public, so I called and registered about twenty five men from our group. Several days later the drug company representative called me to say that the doctor felt we knew too much about PCa and that he had requested that men from the support group not attend. He felt that we might embarrass him. This was crazy, we are not out to embarrass or to get anybody, especially the doctors. All we want to do is share information. Needless to say we don't go where we are not wanted and did not attend that meeting. That doctor lost a lot of points with our Man to Man support group.

In all fairness to the doctors, at the present time we are getting some referrals from the oncologists and urologists and some radiologists. Several of them have been our guest speakers and realized we do give out good information and are really making their job easier.

The local doctors who spoke at our meetings were Dr. Salevitz (urologist); Dr. Burke, and Dr. Kim and Dr. Popadopolous (radiation oncologists) and Dr. Agoliati (oncologist) who by the way did a great job at our last lecture. Dr. Agoliati discussed diet, environment, pesticides. He made a point of how breast and prostate cancer are very similar.

All of the Doctors did a fine job and we look forward to having them speak again; I can assure you that no one was embarrassed, the group or the doctors.

I could go on and on raving about our support group but I will let you decide how important it is by having the men themselves tell you their stories and what the group did for them and their families in their fight against prostate cancer.

In my opinion and theirs, joining a support group makes sense. Join one and you will live longer and happier, it is a proven scientific fact.

ACHES AND PAINS

Dennis and I, Jules may not be doctors, but we have witnessed over 50 sessions of Man to Man meetings and it seems as though every man who was diagnosed with PCa has had or does have aches and pains. A big advantage of our support group is we are very informal and the men feel comfortable discussing any aspect of this disease. Aches, pains and inconvenience such as bathroom problems are freely discussed.

We have one man who is in his late seventies, and is resentful over aftereffects from his radiation treatments. These problems apparently can not be corrected. Those of us who are regulars have heard his story many times. This is OK because he obviously feels better after getting this off his chest and making people feel better is one reason our support group is here.

Most frequent complaints; Hot flashes, usually from someone who is on CHT. Almost everything imaginable has been mentioned. Numbness of legs, stiffness of back, aching of shins and joints and other parts. Bathroom problems, mainly frequent urination.

If a man is on some kind of treatment or has just completed treatment, the discomfort could be caused by this and may eventually go away. It's possible that the problem is not related to PCa. For example a man could be stiff just from getting older perhaps a touch of arthritis.

A man at a support group meeting will feel better seeing that others have the same problem and that it is not unusual. If there is a bad reaction during treatment, sometimes the treatment is stopped. A good example is the hormone Eulexin. Sometimes this drug causes damage to the liver. Sometimes there is medication that can offset certain drug induced problems, like hot flashes.

We mentioned early in this book that a patient should be advised by his doctor about any possible aftereffects of proposed drugs. Many times a man who is aging will become more interested in his quality of life, as opposed to his longevity.

JS

As for myself, Dennis I found a phrase in the Bible, Ecclesiastes, Chapter 12, Verse One. It tells all about people involved in the support groups, "If thou do good, know to whom thou dost it, and there shall be much thanks for thy good deeds." As I said in my biography I feel God has blessed me with my bout of PCa. I have met men who are of great fame and most who aren't, but we all put our underwear on the same way, one leg at a time and PCa brings us all to the same level, or status.

My son Brian wrote a poem for me Christmas, 1995 while he was inspired by reading in the Bible, 2 Corinthians, Chapter 12 Verse 7 through 10.

The Thorn in My Side
Here I am
Day by Day
My life set before
me as I pray.
Some will soar, and touch the sky.
But mine is given another way.
I have a thorn in my side
God has allowed to remain
that I may grow stronger
-Not in vain.
It keeps me on the path.
It keeps Me strong
I think I now know
Why He's left it so long.
-So I depend on him more,
And give thanks for God's grace;
for the thorn in my side

Brian S. O'Hara

This inspires me to continue helping through the support group.

SUMMARY (Jules)

Our Man to Man, support group has now been in existence over four years and has exceeded all expectations. Over 300 men have attended at least one meeting.

At every meeting pertinent information is handed out. Some of it comes from computers that at least a few of our men have. One member has organized a library so that he can answer almost any question.

We have all kinds of speakers: On drugs, holistic medicine, diet, therapy and chiropractic care. We have had a lawyer, radiologist, urologist, oncologist and even an expert on Lyme disease. Having PCa does not guarantee that a person will never have any other illness.

At a typical meeting we start off by introducing the new men. There are usually about six. Each man gives his story, then he is given suggestions by the "veterans." These new men are probably the main beneficiaries of the group. They obtain a lot of information that the old timers did not have access to.

Here is a good example: Recently a new man was considering radiation. Six members who had this treatment each related their experience. They had generally done well although some had complications. Three out of the six said if they had it to do over, they would opt not to have the radiation. Everyone is open because we are all in the same boat. The only regret some members have is that they did not attend the meeting sooner.

Practically every man mentions how valuable the support group has been for him. There are always new developments. No matter how good a person's prognosis, no one has a guarantee that there will not be a recurrence.

Therefore, no matter how good things are or appear to be, it can never hurt to keep up with the latest news.

As Dennis mentioned earlier, the tone of the meetings is definitely upbeat. Nevertheless, in the back of everyone's mind is the fact that this is "hardball." No matter how good it looks, the stakes are high. What is on the line here is one's very life.

It's a known fact that participants in support groups live longer. The groups have proven their worth. People like Dennis who put themselves out to organize and manage a support group perform an invaluable service for their fellow man.

SIDE BY SIDE — Jackie O'Hara

I started SIDE by SIDE because of my husband (Dennis O'Hara) gentle insistence that I do something to help the ladies, whose husbands, male partners or friends who have prostate cancer.

Basically I am a very quiet introverted person and when Dennis, or Iggy as I have always called him, asked me to head up Side by Side, I told him, "You have to be kidding and you are crazy" or something to that affect.

Since I had accompanied him earlier to American Cancer Society headquarters, to learn how to be a facilitator, my argument that I could not do this went down the tubes. I was qualified in their eyes because we had trained together.

With a lot of reservation I agreed to do it and Iggy agreed that if it did not work I could quit.

He is always getting me into trouble like this, trying to involve me in all sorts of life's embarrassing situations; sometimes I agree and most of the time they work out. But this, to be a leader of a women's support group for survivors of prostate cancer, my gosh what does he want from me now!

At that time we had been married over 26 years and prior to our marriage we had dated and now have known each other a total of over 37 years. He is always challenging me with new things to do, like going camping and one year even driving to Alaska with our three little ones, and let's go here and let's do this and that.

I felt a little challenged at his request for me to become a facilitator; most of the times these different situations worked out, but this Side by Side really got my dander up. Like him, the only group I had started was my 3 children and at times I had second thoughts on how successful that group had been.

I finally said yes because of Iggy's continued gentle pressure. I had been coping with his prostate cancer by my silence and trying to handle it on my own. My fears were naturally of his dying and then being left alone in this world, at age 48 with three grown children still at home. Because of the lack of knowledge about prostate cancer, I did not know how long he would survive.

I did and still continue to worry about his possible pain and suffering that someday may happen and what role I would play in helping him and our family through it all.

Side by Side has given me some relief in this area because I see other women who are very strong and courageous and I draw from their strength and courage.

Side by Side has been in existence for over 4 years now. We meet in a small but close group of female members of prostate cancer survivors, and maintain a very relaxed atmosphere. We talk not only about cancer, (most of the women in the group are very knowledgeable on the subject of PCa) but we also talk about diet and nutrition and life in general.

Whenever a new member comes to our meetings we pay very special attention to them giving them the floor first and trying to calm their fears by listening to them and letting them express themselves by letting it all out.

I always assure them that their husbands or significant other is in the next room gaining much knowledge and gathering a tremendous amount of information from the Man to Man group. This will enable them to make a proper decision that will be best for his particular needs.

He will be armed with all the medical terms the doctors have used, and will not be confused anymore. Most of all he and you can sit down together with your doctor and make a choice of treatment that is best for both of you. Because of Side by Side and Man to Man you will not be alone anymore or as afraid as you both have been.

The reason I continue to facilitate or lead this group is the improvement I see in the women when they return for another meeting; they are more able to cope. I can see the calmness that comes over them compared to how they were at the first meeting, because of what they and their husbands have learned at our meetings.

I went for a long period of time being in fear of the unknown future of my husband's PCa. Now because of Side by Side and Man to Man it is not necessary for us to go through this awful dark time of loneliness and fear and confusion about our male counterparts.

At one particular meeting recently I put a question to the women. The question was, "How are you coping with your husbands cancer?" It went around the table and that's when I discovered how strong and courageous they are due to the fact that most of them are coping exceptionally well because of the support and information they have obtained from Side by Side and Man to Man.

That was when I realized that Side by Side is not a chore for me anymore and I don't dread the meetings at all.

If your husband or male partner, friend, father or brother is diagnosed with PCa, or has PCa, go to a Side by Side or a Man to Man groups meeting get involved and arm yourself with all the facts on prostate cancer. See how we are doing and draw on our strength and courage as I did. You will definitely feel better and he will live longer seeing that your stress and anxiety levels have diminished.

I will continue to facilitate Side by Side and I thank all the women and the American Cancer Society for the opportunity to help others cope with the stress of prostate cancer.

Our daughters and our son see how my husband and I are coping with the cancer, they see we are not flipping out all the time about cancer. They hear me on the phone with both ladies and men, giving them support and information and they know we are doing OK.

Sometimes I would like to forget about cancer because it gets to me now and then. My husband is always on the phone constantly talking to people, organizations and groups about prostate cancer and I get mad! But then I realize there is a need for the support groups and that he and I must continue to carry the torch and keep the flame lit. We must pass on our knowledge and support to others so that they are not in the dark and frightening stages of life alone.

I know we would all like to forget about cancer, but to do so, may jeopardize our lives. Cancer becomes a family affair. We should keep informed of the newest treatments available for the particular type of cancer that we are involved with.

Support
Group
Interviews

"You are your own best doctor."

—Dr. Albert Schweitzer

Be the captain of your own health team. Question, read, experiment, always with prudence, and seek other medical opinions.

INTRODUCTION TO INTERVIEWS

There are no two cases exactly alike. Here we cover just about every possible situation. There are cases where the man had little information, perhaps there was no Man to Man support group available to him at that time. Some men acted hastily and with little information, but have apparently lucked out so to speak, and done the right thing. This certainly seems to be the case with my co-author, Dennis O'Hara. He has now gone over 5 years since his radical prostatectomy and he is OK. We pray that he stays that way.

On the other hand, many of these men regret having opted for the wrong treatment. In some cases the person was attending Man to Man meetings and the information was available, but he still acted hastily and incorrectly.

With or without Man to Man, it seems like some people are not interested in obtaining a lot of information. They just know they want something unpleasant removed from their body as quickly as possible.

Some new men come to a meeting knowing next to nothing. Others have read up on the subject of PCa, consulted a number of doctors and are very well informed.

Any newly diagnosed person can read the following interviews and take note, where there are good examples to follow. Where someone did everything wrong and what not to do. Through the cooperation of these men who were interviewed, many will undoubtedly be helped.

Interview 1

This statement is taken from RAM, age 69. My earliest symptoms, which I didn't realize were associated with prostate cancer, were back aches, lower back aches and also my hips gave me a lot of problems; I couldn't stand in one position for more then a few minutes. I thought it was associated with my job, as I used to climb poles at one time, as an employee of a local telephone company. I did not pay too much attention to it. I had an appointment for my annual physical and through the course of the examination, I told my doctor I was having these backaches.

My doctor told me he would check it out. He continued on with the next part of the physical, a Digital Rectal Exam, (DRE). He told me "I feel something abnormal on your prostate."

I was 56 years old then. The doctor recommended I see a urologist to further check me out, and he gave me the name and made the appointment for me.

About a week or ten days later I had that appointment with the urologist. He also gave me the DRE and he verified what my regular doctor had thought he had discovered, there were some irregularities in the shape of my prostate. He then stated a biopsy of my prostate should be done. This was in 1983 and the famous PSA (Prostate Specific Antigen) blood test was not popular yet.

The biopsy was performed in the hospital about two weeks after the DRE. It was not very uncomfortable for me, since I was given a local anesthetic. Of course it was not ultra sound guided as it is done today.

About a week or ten days later I went back to my doctors office with my wife. He told us that he "had some bad news." I asked him what it was and he said "You have prostate cancer. I picked up a positive biopsy in one of the quadrants of the prostate."

Several minutes went by; my wife and I were in complete shock about the findings, and I finally asked the urologist "What do we do now?" The doctor then said "You do have a couple of options, one being an orchiectomy which is the surgical removal of the testicles or, have the prostate removed (radical prostatectomy "RP") or, you can have the seed implant treatment."

I asked him what is the least invasive treatment because I did not want to be cut, I have been cut in the past and I really wasn't looking forward to having another operation unless it really was necessary.

The doctor then said that the seeds would be best for me under the circumstances and that he did not know how effective it would be in my case. He also said "I will give it a try anyway."

At this point I did not know what my PSA was, I don't even know if he took one, because he never mentioned any numbers to me. The doctor stated that the cancer looked pretty well defined and not a very aggressive cancer, still he could not guarantee me anything as far as the outcome of the seed implantation was concerned.

My wife and I decided the seed implants were the least invasive and that we would go for it. All the pre-op tests which consisted of Bone and CAT scans, chest X-ray, showed no spread of cancer.

On March 2, 1983 the seeds were implanted by a doctor in Westchester County N.Y. He cut me down the middle, belly button to penis and then inserted the seeds, 36 in all, into the prostate. This was all done in the blind as the Ultra Sound Guided procedure used today was not yet popular. Also, as part of the procedure the doctor told me "I had to tie up the Lymph Nodes so no radiation would escape and get into them and travel through my system." Maybe he meant if one of the seeds escaped.

I stayed a total of 13 days in the hospital and then went home to recover.

After a few days at home, I noticed I was passing some of the seeds through my urine into the toilet bowl, I lost ten of the seeds in all.

I called the doctor and told him what was happening. He told me to keep an eye on things for a while, to use a strainer he had given me, to catch the seeds in case I pass any more of them. He also told me if indeed I did pass some more of the seeds there would be a problem. I often wondered what he was going to do if I did pass anymore and catch them into the strainer. Would he use them again. Or could they use them in our local power plant? After all they were radioactive. As it turned out these questions were never answered due to the fact that I never did pass anymore and retained a total of 26 seeds.

Recuperation was long, over three and one half months. When I returned to work I was put on a half day basis for six weeks. The doctor mentioned that I may become incontinent and also that I should not go near any women, especially those who might be pregnant because of the possibility of radiation exposure. I was especially concerned for my daughter's sake, so I told them to stay away from me for at least 6 months.

After six months or so I returned to work on full duty. I was now impotent and incontinent at age 57; this was very tough for me to handle. After a year or so things started to return to normal and I was able to resume my sex life. The incontinent part of it disappeared about the same time.

Yearly checkups were done and everything was going smoothly until one of the checkups revealed that my prostate was enlarged and hard. I am now 64 and eight years have gone by since the seeds were implanted. The PSA is now popular, I had one done and the results were 18, well over the number 4 limit which is the acceptable norm.

The original doctor who did the seed implantation had retired and another urologist had taken his place. He suggested another biopsy be done and I agreed. This time the biopsy was done in his office. I was awake and could hear and feel the clicks as the samples were being taken. A total of eight samples of my prostate were taken.

Several days later we were back in his office and again got the bad news that the cancer was back. "Now what do I do?" was my next question to the doctor. He gave me the same options, orchiectomy, or a radical prostatectomy. He could not give me anymore seeds; however, another possibility was for me to go on a hormone therapy, which consisted of a needle once every month for the rest of my life. My next question was, "How expensive are the hormones?" His answer "Very expensive." I was now 64 years and had been retired for five years.

Since my company's insurance plan would cover the cost of the hormones, I decided to go with the Combined Hormonal Therapy (CHT) which consists of a needle once a month (Lupron) and (Eulexin), which consists of 2 pills every 8 hours, three times a day.

I again asked the doctor how long this treatment would continue to keep the cancer in check and again I got the same answer, "I can't guarantee anything, we will do it for as long as we can then take the next step if necessary."

After being on the Combined Hormonal Therapy, for six months my PSA dropped down from 18 to 1.6 and then went down to 1.

During all this my wife and I had decided to relocate. We moved from Westchester County to Dutchess County. Traveling back and forth to the doctors was beginning to take its toll on us, especially when I had to make that trip during a kidney stone attack.

Because of the above reasons, in 1994 I picked a Urology group in Poughkeepsie N.Y.

Before the support group I was completely ignorant about prostate cancer. I still would have made the same choices. I feel very lucky in the choices I made because, I could have had my prostate removed, and I don't know how my quality of life would have been affected.

Coming to the support group turned my whole life around. It made me more knowledgeable, more inclined not to be afraid of what I did not know. Now I have become very educated about my condition. Seeing other men in different stages of prostate cancer gave me hope, I found that my problems are nothing compared to what some of the men are going through. Even to this day I find every meeting to be an education. Learning something new or improved about my particular situation just makes you more able to take care of your own problems. The group provides the kind of support I need to just keep going.

At every meeting I learn more and more. For instance, I first learned of the Intermittent Hormonal Treatment (or as some doctors call it PULSE THERAPY) at one of our meetings. By the way Dennis O'Hara, was one of the first people to talk about this at one of the support group meetings. After hearing this suddenly, I said to myself, "What is this and am I eligible for something like this?" After talking to Dennis and listening to some of the other men who were bringing information into the group, it really started me thinking about it.

I finally asked the urologist who I had been seeing locally about the concept of Intermittent Hormonal Therapy; he was dead set against it. This was the determining factor that caused me to change doctors.

For those of you who don't know what the Intermittent Hormone Therapy consists of, I will explain! After a period of time on the Hormones the cancer will not be fooled anymore, and will continue to grow. This usually happens after eighteen months to two years. By going off the Hormones and closely watching the PSA, should it start to rise and continue to rise you simply start the Hormones again. This just seems like simple logic to me and we at the group know many cases where this is working and thus it prolongs the use of the hormones. Some doctors disagree and feel the cancer comes back very aggressive but we haven't seen that proof yet.

The urologist I had been seeing felt I did not know enough about this sort of therapy treatment, but he was wrong, so I sought out another doctor. I chose a local oncologist. We discussed the intermittent therapy and decided to go ahead with this. He felt that I had the knowledge and the group had provided me with the necessary information to make a rational decision on the form of treatment I wanted.

At that time I was on Lupron injections alone and my PSA started to rise from point one to two points or so. The oncologist suggested I go on Eulexin with Lupron. I told him I did not want to go on Eulexin because it consisted of taking 2 capsules every 8 hours and also had some bad side effects, one being your liver enzymes can become elevated. I had heard much better things about the Casodex from the support group at our meetings.

The doctor had just heard of Casodex, he agreed with me. As a matter of fact I was the first guy in the group to start taking it. Even my pharmacist was not aware of it and had to special order it for me. It took them several days to get it. So once again, our Man to Man group had scooped the medical community with a new form of treatment for PCa. I would say we are on the forefront of information when it comes to PCa. After all this is our lives and our quality of life that we are dealing with here.

The Lupron and the Casodex knocked my PSA right down to point one. I started the Intermittent Hormonal Therapy April, 1996. That was my last injection of Lupron. I also stopped the Casodex on that date. Two months after I started this new therapy my PSA was still point one. My doctor has recommended a PSA every two months while I am on pulse therapy. We also have discussed in great length what if the PSA should start to rise. At what number would we restart the regular Combined Hormonal Therapy. We have decided to cross that bridge when we come to it.

Of course I am going to listen to my doctor, but I can assure you that our group and their input will also play a big part in my decision. It is very important for me not to panic. The group's knowledge and support will not allow this to happen.

As far as my wife is concerned Man to Man and Side by Side, provide us both with a lot of good information and emotional support. She attends the meetings regularly and gets a lot of support from the other women. We both definitely agree these two groups have changed our lives and the way we deal with my PCa.

My wife and I also like the idea of separate meetings. We both feel that there are very private moments and emotions which we could not share if the meetings were mixed. We like the idea of mixed meetings when we have guest speakers.

When I walk into the room with all the men present I feel almost like we are family because of what we have and share. When we have new members come in we can listen to their stories and we can provide some kind of a guidance to them. You know it and I know it; we have seen guys come into our meetings who are crying, literally crying, practically basket cases, then all of a sudden its like a new world to them because the support group is there for them. You know it's like the old Indian saying "You don't know how it is till you walk in my moccasins."   —RAM

Update Feb. 1998: Went back on CHT Oct. 1996. CHT lasted until April 1997, then resumed pulse therapy and it held until Oct 1997, then back on CHT until Jan 1997. Presently on pulse therapy and awaiting a recent PSA. My PSA throughout the pulse therapy has ranged from a low of .1 to a high of 2.8. I have been averaging 6 months on CHT and 6 months off. Pretty good as far as I am concerned. This gives me a little breather from the CHT and prolongs the life of the Hormonal Therapy.

Interview 2

I am presently 68 years old. I did not have any symptoms at all to make me feel I had prostate cancer. I had made up my mind to retire at age 65. I went to my regular GP (general practitioner) for a check up. He suggested because of my age to have a PSA blood test done. I never had this before.

I had the blood test and the results came back 10. The GP had always given me a Digital Rectal Exam (DRE) but it was always just a matter of fact. He never really probed and gave much time to the DRE. The whole thing lasted a short time.

The reason I say this is because, after the PSA, my GP suggested I see a urologist; I did, and during the DRE, he really felt my prostate gland. My gosh I thought his finger was going to come out of my teeth. There was pain when he did the procedure. When I walked out of there, I thought to myself, this guy has the fingers of a gibbon (a slender, long-armed arboreal anthropoid ape), it felt like he was up in my throat. After the examination the doctor said to me, "There is something I feel and it's not normal." You see, urologists unlike GP's are more familiar with the prostate, how it feels and its texture, etc. Let me make a suggestion here, when it comes to a prostate exam, go to a urologist, not your regular doctor.

Because of my abnormal PSA and DRE, the urologist felt a biopsy was next in line for me. The biopsy was done at the local urologist's office. I think there were a total of 4 probes and not any great particular discomfort felt by me. I was watching the whole procedure on the monitor and I did feel the sharp pain when samples were taken, but it was no big deal. After the biopsy I did have some blood in my semen (sperm) and also in my urine, but it only lasted about 10 days.

After the biopsy my sexual function was effected. I don't know whether it was psychological or physiological, but from that point on I have experienced erectile dysfunction. I do experience nocturnal erections, but as soon as I am aware of it, it subsides. It is most likely in my mind, but it has lasted for as long as the biopsy was done and that is over 4 years. I do intend to see some out-of- town urologists, who were at one of our meetings who are experts in erectile dysfunction.

Getting back to the biopsy and its results, which was cancer of the prostate, stage B2. I decided to have a second opinion. The doctor agreed and I spoke to a friend of mine who is a dentist. He set up a second opinion for me at a hospital in Boston, Mass.

I went to Boston and met with the doctor. He did his examination and then we sat down to have a talk, not with the doctor who did the actual exam, but with the head of the urology department at this hospital. He had all my records from my local urologist. After his review of all the records and the exam made by his associate, he concurred with the diagnosis of prostate cancer at stage B2.

Because of my heart condition (angina), surgery was out of the question. Both he and my urologist felt external beam radiation was the way for me to go. I kind of feel that both doctors felt this way because of the blood loss involved, the length of time that a radical procedure takes to do and my heart condition would put me at great risk.

No other options were discussed and at that time I don't think I was a part of our Man to Man support group yet. I came to the meetings starting in August of 1993, and I had already started with the hormones to shrink the cancer prior to the radiation. I was on that about two months before I went to the first support group meeting.

I don't recall how I discovered Man to Man, but I had heard about it from someone. I had already made up my mind about the radiation, so any information I picked up at the meetings did not sway me one way or another. Don't forget, we were then in the very beginning of our support group and the information we had at that time was very limited.

I went for a total of 36 radiation treatments done by a linear accelerator, this was one of the stipulations made by the doctor in Boston. He said not to have cobalt treatments. Evidently most of the problems associated with radiation came from cobalt treatments, because they were not able to direct the beam or pinpoint the target like a linear accelerator can today.

Now, when they identify the target they use a probe that goes into your rectum similar to a biopsy probe. They are able to see the prostate and they get a skeletal readout just like 3D (three dimensional). All this information is fed into the computer. This is done on the first visit. They actually have a mold that is created just for your anatomy. Then they measure and tattoo you, so to speak with a black dot (which by the way I still have on my body after four years). They do these marks on three sides of your body, your stomach and both sides. Then when you are lined up properly on these spots you are told "do not move," and no matter what I had to do I did not move because all the coordinates were lined up. I often wonder about the other men in our support group; maybe they moved and that is why they are experiencing so much trouble with the after effects of their radiation.

Getting back to the tattoos, they prick you with a little pin, insert a dye which then becomes a permanent mark for reference. They look like little beauty marks. I still have them on my body.

I have done quite well on radiation compared to some of the other fellows in our group. I don't remember if I was warned about the fact that I might have this or that reaction but I had absolutely nothing. I might have had some diarrhea but that could have been from the Eulexin, the hormonal therapy, but the diarrhea did not last very long anyway. It was very minor and not a bother to me at all. I did lose some pubic hair, which soon grew back.

In November of 1997 it will be four years since the completion of the external beam radiation treatments. My PSA went from 10 to 0.5. In three years, my PSA has gone up to 1.8 as of August 1996. I do have an appointment with the urologist to discuss what the rise in PSA means and if anything should be done about it.

Another problem I am having is a burning sensation upon ejaculation, it is very uncomfortable and annoying. Another thing is if I have to urinate, I now feel it in the groin area, again it is not a pain, but it too is uncomfortable. I also have discomfort in the groin area, but after a bowel movement all seems well.

To date, I have not had any follow up tests such as chest -X-ray or Bone scan, just a PSA every three or four months. I am experiencing some minor aches and pains when I get up in the morning, like a tight feeling in my joints, maybe its old age creeping up on me, as I am now 68 years old. But as soon as I move around its fine. You know you start thinking bone involvement, but if the PCa was there the pain would not go away with activity. If it did not go away with activity I would then ask the doctor for a Bone scan.

As far as my angina, my family has talked me into an exercise program so I can get into shape and keep myself fit. I can live with the angina, I take Ismo twice daily for the pain, and I am doing the exercises in the gym. The Ismo is a slow release of nitroglycerine.

I attend the Man to Man meetings whenever I am at home. I like to go there for knowledge and information that is shared and basically to help other guys. After all I am on the other side of the spectrum. Most of the men have had RP's. I was one of the lucky ones very successful with radiation. It might be a good thing for the new people to know that it is possible for them to have a good experience with external beam radiation, without going through all the bad aftereffects. Up to this point my radiation was very very easy.

I never did have any incontinent problems prior to or after radiation, but partial impotence still remains. Don't get me wrong. It is working, but it may still be in my mind, about being able to perform, as I said before I am going to see an erectile dysfunction expert.

As far as finding the meetings depressing, prostate cancer is a downer to begin with. How can you say to a bunch of guys, "We have this problem so lets go out and celebrate." That's a lot of BS. You (Dennis) are doing a good service and we all have seen the results. The comments from the men themselves are very encouraging.

My wife L enjoys Side by Side tremendously as all the women do and she also gets a lot of information on nutrition etc. from their meetings. They share the heart-breaks and when there is a good report they have happy times. She is finding out a lot about the women's problems and how they cope, etc. You know, they suffer right along with us through this ordeal and both Man to Man and Side by Side help us get through it.

As far as separate meetings, I like that concept very much, because we men talk about our manhood, or our lack of our manhood and most of us don't want to share that with strange ladies. They do join us from time to time when we have guest speakers and it seems to work out alright.

We get to know each other at the survivors day picnics and when we have our recognition dinners. I know we have a partial mixed meeting from time to time so the ladies can put names and faces together and we can get to know each other.

Summing it all up, if you are diagnosed with PCa or any disease, join a support group, so you and your spouse can become informed. Besides that, you will also meet some very nice people and you will become a survivor like we are.

Update April, 1997

In 7 months, my PSA has accelerated from 1.8 to 5.5. A Bone scan and other tests revealed no abnormalities. The sudden rise in PSA was a concern to the urologist. We have decided to go on the Combined Hormonal Therapy.

I presently take one Casodex pill per day, and a Lupron injection every 28 days. Future treatment will be determined by my response to present therapy. As of Nov. 1997, PSA is less then 0.1. In January of 1998 I will discuss with the urologist possibly going on intermittent hormonal therapy.   — CK

Interview 3

My name is AC and right now I am 59 years old. Believe it or not, I had no symptoms whatsoever to alert me to the fact that I might have a problem with my prostate. I did have frequent urination on occasion, but I attributed that to the drinking of excess fluids and I did not think too much of it.

I really did not have any problems with my plumbing parts at all. I did have some back problems, but I thought this was from previous back injuries I had sustained as a hard working laborer, but much to my surprise I did find out later, it could have been prostate cancer.

I had been going to my regular doctor for over 20 years and he had been examining me every year including a Digital Rectal Exam (DRE). They were always very fast and it felt like it was a friend of mine performing the procedure. It always went easy, no discomfort at all and everything was always fine. He never thought about giving a PSA blood test, which tells you how much PSA your prostate is putting out. To date anything over 4 is questionable.

I became upset with this doctor after hearing about the PSA from friends and went to a local doctor. He gave me a PSA and a DRE. Within one week I found out that I had a reading of 7.

From there I went to see a local urologist. He gave me another DRE, which was really a much more involved examination of my prostate. After a two week waiting period, another PSA was given. The doctor told me that I had to wait the two weeks because the prostate gland was stimulated now and it could give a false reading if the two week waiting period was not followed. This PSA was down to 6.7.

The urologist suggested a biopsy of the prostate be done in light of how the PSA was behaving, plus his conclusions from the DRE. About two weeks later the biopsy was done in his office. I tolerated it very well and did not find it to be a problem at all. I remember watching it on the TV monitor and feeling the specimens being taken. I think it was four or five samples taken from my prostate.

I had no post biopsy problems at all. Two weeks went by and my wife and I had an appointment to see the urologist. He informed us that from the biopsy samples, the pathology report had come back; two of them were positive, and that I had prostate cancer. We talked a little about what to do. He suggested surgery and we went along with his suggestion. A date for the operation was set, it was for July 26, 1994.

My wife and I were not very happy how the doctor had handled this part of it. He never asked what we thought, but just came out and told us that I needed an operation.

Several nights later I was playing cards with some friends and I mentioned to them about my impending surgery. One of the fellows told me about the doctors at Johns Hopkins Hospital in Maryland and about Dr. Walsh, who is the top guy when it comes to prostate surgery. He invented the nerve sparing technique, and does hundreds of radical prostatectomies a year.

They also suggested that I go to John Hopkins Hospital, because they do over 50 or more of these kinds of operations a month. Why take a chance with the local guys who only do about 5 RP's a month. This made a lot of sense to my wife and I.

I did take this advice; my friend gave me all the phone numbers and names of people to talk to. I called Johns Hopkins and made an appointment to see one of the urologist there. He is an associate of Dr. Walsh.

The local urologist had mentioned that there was a man in my area that had started a prostate cancer support group his name was Dennis O'Hara. At about the same time I had made up my mind about going to Johns Hopkins, I called Dennis O'Hara.

My wife and I spoke to both Dennis and his wife Jackie, for a very long time. We discussed many, many things, including some of my options the doctors never mentioned. Most of the pre-operation and post-operation procedures and problems. Believe it or not it was the greatest thing in the world for my wife and I to talk to these two people. It made us feel fantastic and gave us the courage to go through with what was going to take place in our lives. I can truly say that meeting Dennis and Jackie and the others in our support group has been a great inspiration to us.

After several trips to Johns Hopkins, we had a surgery date set up for August 3, 1994. A lot of preparation had to be made prior to this date. After discussions with Dennis, I had decided to give my own blood for the operation. (Which I recommend to anyone contemplating surgery). The blood had to be shipped to Baltimore, which was very expensive to do. I was grateful my insurance company picked up most of the tab for it.

All my medical records had to be sent there, plus I would have to find a doctor locally who would remove the remaining staples, and the foley catheter, (which would be in my penis). The local doctor would have to monitor my progress. My regular doctor agreed to do this.

The day before surgery, my son and my wife trekked off to Baltimore, with a very nervous patient. We arrived five hours later.

The surgery went well; it took about two hours. I did not lose too much blood, as a matter of fact they gave me back one pint the day following surgery and another two pints two days later. Perhaps to make me stronger or whatever. I stayed in the hospital only five days, and nothing dramatic happened while I was there. The pain was under control and all went well.

After I was discharged, my wife and oldest son drove me home. It was a nice ride; I had propped myself up on a bunch of pillows, the 5 hour ride home was not bad at all.

The doctor at Johns Hopkins did discuss the pathology report with us after surgery. He told us the cancer was very close to the edges of my prostate capsule and that in his judgement it might have been out of the capsule already. At that time I did not understand the terms and medical words he was using and did not pay any attention to it. We felt all was OK.

My recuperation period went well. The local doctors took care of the catheter and the remaining staples.

After about 8 months I returned to my heavy work. I was a little incontinent and still impotent at that time. My first PSA after surgery was 0.6 and then 3 months later it was 0.5, then 3 months later it was 0.7. A year after surgery it was now up to 0.9 then it went to 1.2.

I started to get a little concerned with this and tried a little alternative therapy. I ate a lot of garlic, cut out red meats, drank herbal teas, soy, etc. The next PSA was 1.0. Three months later it was up to 2.1.

At one of our support group meetings we had two guest speakers who were urologists. They were not local doctors. I decided to go and talk to one of these doctors. We met and decided to go on Casodex and Proscar. Several weeks later we had another meeting. It was decided to take me off the Proscar which is a drug for Benign Prostatic Hyperplasia,(BPH) an enlarged prostate. He told me that some experiments had been going on using this combination.

He suggested I go on the Combined Hormonal Therapy (CHT) which consisted of a monthly injection of Lupron and a daily pill, Casodex. The doctor told me that if I was his dad, this would be the treatment he would also prescribe.

I went on that treatment and 3 months later my PSA was down to 0.1. As of August 27, 1996 it was 0.1.

As I learned at the support group meetings and talking to you (Dennis) I am now going to try and keep all my blood work at one lab to assure continuity.

I am satisfied with my choice of treatment and really can't blame the doctor for what has happened. I feel he gave me the best operation he could.

Now about our support group. I have learned a lot from Dennis and our group. For instance, I had a chance months ago, to go to the local V.A. Hospital for a second opinion on my choice of treatment. I saw a urologist who told me that after looking over my records and examining me that they were going to **"cure"** me. Well I was taken back, and asked the doctor to explain how they would achieve this. The doctor said they were going to radiate me and this would **"cure"** me. Well I was shocked. Here it was about 18 months since surgery." Where are you going to radiate me," I asked. The doctor said "where your prostate used to be, there in the cavity." I can't tell you what I said to the doctor because of the language I used, but I did ask the doctor, "How do you know that the cancer is there and not somewhere else."

We went round and round for awhile. The doctor was quite amazed at what I knew about prostate cancer, about my treatment, and how it worked. The doctor wanted to know where I got all this knowledge from.

I proudly told the doctor that I was a member of Man to Man, a prostate cancer support group, with over 125 men and we are very well informed about prostate cancer and its different treatments. I also told the doctor there would not be any radiation treatments for me under the present condition I was in, and unless they could prove the cancer was localized in the prostate bed and not spread somewhere else in my body, radiation was a dead issue.

The doctors are always amazed when we men can talk to them in their medical jargon and terminology. After all, we should be well versed on prostate cancer. We are the ones who could die. We should be up on everything, and we do get this from our support group. That's the reason I would not fool around with radiation now, because of what I learned at our meetings.

I attend the meetings regularly because of all the good information that is given both verbally and with handouts. I always felt I was going to beat this cancer stuff and Man to Man has helped me do this. Just being with the men makes me feel relaxed and under no tension. Being at these meetings for the last three years has been great for me and I have learned a lot.

Although my wife does not attend the Side by Side group she supports my going to Man to Man and one of these days I will get her to go.

Looking back I might have made some different choices such as going for the PSA RT-PCR: (PSA reverse transcriptase-polymerase chain reaction, not available as of 2/1997) which is another form of PSA that can detect micrometastatic cells circulating in the blood stream, and can be useful as a screening tool to help avoid unnecessary invasive treatments. It is not FDA approved but used in many locations where clinical trials are being held. The latest technique, which is FDA approved, called ProstaScint, is like a Bone scan but better. It can pinpoint cancer that has spread out of the capsule and it can also tell you where it is, then they can treat you at that site of metastasis. This new method has just been approved by the FDA as of late October 1996. I might have just chosen to go on the Combined Hormonal Therapy 3 to 6 months prior to surgery to shrink the tumor and perhaps the cancer would not have gotten out of the capsule. Some doctors around here don't want to hear about any of this stuff yet but we men at the support group will persist, and because of our good information we will prevail. I understand that at Memorial Sloan Kettering, in NYC, there is now a study going on about the CHT, prior to treatment. This therapy is called Neo Adjuvant Therapy.

I certainly will continue my connection with our group. I will tell everyone I know about it and the wonderful things they do for men who have PCa.

My condition continues to improve. My present PSA Dec. 1997 is less then <0.1 As far as my incontinence is concerned I still wet myself from time to time, mostly stress related and my sex life is under control by using a hand held pump. There are many other methods to help you with your sex problems but we chose this one. It seems to be the easiest. I understand that very soon there may be a pill that we can take for erections as opposed to injections or using an implant.

Don't give up, join a support group meet leaders like Dennis and Jackie and many other fine people, get educated and stay alive. —AC

Interview 4

My age at present is 67 years old, and I didn't have any symptoms regarding prostate cancer. I had gone to my regular MD for my yearly exam, which by the way was two years late. The MD did his exam. At the end of it he told me that I had some blood in my urine and that I should see someone about it. I decided to go to an out of town MD and hospital. After all the lab tests were done it was discovered that I had two Melanomas, one on each side of the bladder, where the kidneys empty into the bladder.

During a surgical procedure these were scraped off my bladder and after a two day stay at the hospital I was released. There also was a catheter inserted up through my urinary canal and up into the kidney so that the scar tissue from the scraping of the bladder would not block the flow of urine. The end of this tube was attached to my penis and I was instructed by the doctor, that at the end of three weeks, to just pull out the tube, which I did and the operation was pronounced a success.

I would then go back to the hospital every 3 months for a year and they would check everything out. During one of the follow-up visits for the bladder I had a Digital Rectal Exam; this was about two years into the whole bladder deal. The MD who was doing the DRE, told me he would like to have me take a PSA blood test. He didn't seem urgent about it and the PSA completely slipped my mind. The next time I went for the bladder checkup, which consists of a cystoscopy (they insert a wire into your penis and it has a opening at the end so that they can look around into your urinary tract etc.), the doctor asked me if I had gotten the PSA, I told him that I had forgotten all about it.

He told me that he wanted me to go downstairs immediately and have a CAT scan of my vital organs and an ultra sound taken of my prostate which I did.

About a week later he called me at home and told me that I had prostate cancer and that I was in stage D2 (cancer cells have gone from the lymph nodes to the bones) and that there was no use in doing a biopsy probe of the prostate, because the cancer had already broken out of my prostate capsule.

The doctor then told me that my next course of action would be to start the Combined Hormonal Therapy (CHT), to try and contain the cancer. The PSA at that time was 332.

The CHT, which was a monthly injection of Lupron and Eulexin, 6 pills a day 2 every 8 hours was immediately started. My PSA dropped down to 3, then 2, then 1 over a period of a year. Then in July of 1996 my last PSA was .03 a very dramatic decrease from the original PSA of 332.

At one time it did go from .02 to .03 but I had gone from the Eulexin to the Casodex (only one pill a day) and we switched back to the Eulexin to see if this made any change in the PSA; it didn't.

The thing that I really can't understand till this day is while I was in the hospital for the Melanoma of the bladder (bladder can-cer) is how a prostate condition could have escaped detection by the doctors. (This particular hospital is a teaching institution). It seemed like everybody who saw me there, instead of shaking my hand and saying hello, they would put their finger into my rectum and give me a DRE. Sometimes I feel as if I was used as a guinea pig.

I don't know if they ever did a PSA in the hospital; I am going to get my records from the hospital and look back and see if they ever did do a PSA.

There was another time when I was told that I had to go back into the hospital for the removal of some more growth on the bladder and when I went into the operating room, I was given a spinal and sedated.

The doctor, plus three interns or students were there; when I woke up the doctor told me that everything was fine and nothing had been done because everything was OK. I am not so sure about this either. I feel the procedure was just an exploratory one using me as a guinea pig.

The hospital and the doctor who is a urologist both have very good reputations and I hate to believe that I was used as a study example for learning doctors.

Another thing that bothers me is why after all the DRE exams I had at this teaching hospital that no one came up with my prostate problems until it became a stage D2 which is a condition that is kind of tough to contain.

When I got the news of my prostate cancer it was devastating. People hear the word devastating and people pass it off, they say yeah that's devastating but when you are told you have PCa and the only knowledge you have about it is that it is a killer you really get scared and really relate to the word devastating.

I went into complete emotional shock, plus male menopause at the same time, caused by the hormone treatments, which suppressed my male hormones. I was really in bad shape and very depressed. I tried to sleep it away and I could not talk without crying. I feel anything that can affect your physical well being can really take its toll on you emotionally.

I would like to believe from here on that I am going to survive this war with prostate cancer. The way I feel today I am sure of it.

You must talk to your doctor. The last time I talked to my doctor he told me I had three good years. I am into my third good year now. Does that mean after the third good year I am going to go down the drain?

When I asked him, he told me he could not guarantee I was going to be in the 80 percent that last five years. I failed to ask if I am in the longevity part of the five years, or the short end of it.

I have a friend, who has been on CHT for 15 years, this is very encouraging to me as well as all of us who are on CHT.

I have heard about the intermittent hormonal therapy through Man to Man. I have not considered it yet. I did mention it to my doctor about two and a half years ago and nothing has come of it. I will keep it in the back of my mind for future reference.

I discovered Man to Man support group in the local newspaper. I saw a small ad about the meeting. I could not wait to get down there to meet men like myself. Let me tell you that when I walked out of that room after the first meeting I was a totally different man. There were other fellows in the room who were in the same boat I was. Here they were functioning and living productive lives. They were talking and giving me some very good suggestions. I finally felt after that first meeting, I did indeed have a future.

I remember talking to you (Dennis) on the phone for very long periods of time, at least two or three different times. You had told me all about the support group and how important it was for me to attend the meetings.

I really had reached the end of my rope emotionally and I was becoming very unstable about continuing life. In my opinion the Man to Man meetings are a must for anyone who has prostate cancer. We need help and we need to talk to people who know what they are talking about. Our support group provides that knowledge and fellowship.

I believe that our Man to Man support group, provides better counseling then any doctor, or psychologist. There is more collective knowledge in our group then you can get from your 15 minute appointment with your MD, who at the end of the 15 minutes has to rush off to the next patient.

Looking back at the whole ordeal, now that I am a member of Man to Man and our support group, I definitely would have done things differently. For instance, I would have demanded a PSA the first time I had my regular exam with my MD. I certainly would have made sure they gave me a PSA in the hospital, at the very first sign of the bladder cancer.

I would have insisted on a complete work up of my prostate if I knew then what I know now. I feel the PSA should be a mandatory procedure while you are in the hospital with any urinary problems whatsoever. You know, I never did ask the urologist why he did not order a PSA while I was in the hospital for the bladder cancer. Someday I will ask him. He probably will tell me it was just a human error.

I do not find anything negative about our Man to Man support group, the only thing I feel there may be a need for is going from one meeting a month back to the two meetings a month. I know it is a lot of work for you (Dennis) but sometimes that wait for the month to go by is very long, sometimes the need is very urgent, such as when you're having emotional problems. I was very lucky to catch a meeting very fast.

I had to wait a week for the meeting, it really was awful to have to wait, but being able to call Dennis O'Hara and to talk to him or anybody else you may know who is connected with the group, like Jules Schwartz, (who I know and went to high school with), will fill a great void until you can get to a meeting.

I like the idea of separate meetings without the ladies present and I feel it was a very well thought out procedure to decide on that concept. Men need to talk among themselves. Women while they support us and have to be a part of this prostate cancer, with them present, it can tend to be a confusion factor at times when men are trying to get a point across to each other.

I also believe that the ladies should be included in our meetings every once in a while to keep them abreast of what is going on. Let's face it they are standing right along side of us through it all and we need them.

Dennis, I just think the world of our support group. We really need more exposure in the press. So all men who get diagnosed with PCa, can be aware of the fact that there is good information and help out there. This will help them become survivors like you and I.

It is wonderful that our meetings are in the local newspaper for the general public to know about. It is important that we advocate screenings for our sons, male members of our families, and the general male public over 50 years old, unless there is history of PCa, then it should be done at age 40.

I tell all the males in my family, regardless of their age, to see a urologist, get a prostate screening and a PSA once a year. Early diagnosis can be made and instead of being told as in my case that you are a D2, maybe you will be told you are in the early stages of PCa like stage A or B. It would have made all the difference in my case, I know that now.

Now to get back to you, Jules and Stu and the rest of the men in our group. The best thing to ever happen to a person in my opinion, who has PCa, is to join a Man to Man support group and become educated about your PCa.

I am sure that this book you and Jules are writing will make a lot of men and their families aware of what is out there for them, both good and bad. We need the awareness about our conditions (PCa) and this book will surely make them aware. The average guy should not take the MD's word about PCa. Get a second opinion, insist on a PSA, and obtain all the information you can on prostate cancer, before you get diagnosed.

—DW

Interview 5

My age at the present is 71. I had no symptoms of prostate disease, but in October of 1994 I went to a free prostate screening clinic, sponsored by the American Cancer Society at St. Francis Hospital in Poughkeepsie, N.Y.

The clinic consisted of a Prostate Specific Antigen (PSA) blood test and a Digital Rectal Exam (DRE) exam given by the local urologists. My PSA came back with a reading of 8.8, so I called the urologist who had taken part in the screening and he advised me to come into see him for a consultation, which I did.

At the consultation the doctor recommended that I go for a biopsy of my prostate, which I did in February of 1995. The results came back cancer of the prostate at the B2 stage, (the tumor is still confined to the prostate capsule) with a Gleason score of 5 (Gleason score is a widely used method for classifying the cellular differentiation of cancerous tissues, the numbers go from 1 to 10 and the high numbers indicate poor differentiation and therefore more aggresive cancer).

Two days later I had the pleasure of joining the Man to Man prostate cancer support group. I had seen the ad in the newspaper, I said to myself I will start there and learn everything I can about my prostate cancer.

So I started my research immediately after diagnosis and at the very first meeting of the support group I learned a lot about my condition. I also sent away to PAACT (Patients Advocates for Advanced Cancer Treatment) and after two days I received a packet from them on PCa.

After hearing what the men at the support group had to say and the information from PAACT, I decided to seek a second and third opinion. Upon getting these opinions the doctors and I jointly agreed on what treatment to follow. The treatment chosen was the total Hormonal blockade or CHT (Combined Hormonal Therapy).

I have been on this therapy for close to two years now and it has worked very well for me. My PSA for the last three readings and by the way I take a PSA test every 3 months, has leveled off to 0.0.

At the very last consultation with my doctor in July of 1996, my doctor and I have decided that it would be alright for me to go on the intermittent hormonal therapy, which means that I will be removing myself completely from the Hormones and monitoring the PSA every ninety days. As far as I am concerned this seems to be a reasonable course of action for me to pursue.

As I had said before I had no classic signs of PCa whatsoever, it was picked up by me taking advantage of the free prostate screening, which consisted of the PSA and the DRE. I urge all men to take advantage of this program if it is available in their community.

The biopsy was done in the doctor's office and it was kind of uncomfortable. They do give you two shots for the pain but you can still feel them going in there through the rectum and placing all the instruments. When they took the samples of the prostate tissue, I really felt it. The doctor took a total of 16 samples, because he dropped some of the little slugs of tissues and he had to take more. The procedure was termed a global biopsy because they could not see a solid tumor in any one spot.

Following the biopsy I did have all the tests such as Bone and CAT scans, chest X-ray. Later on when I saw another oncologist for a second opinion, I had a Magnetic Resonance Imaging (MRI). This is a sort of three dimensional view of my prostate, and they used a coil inserted into my rectum to enhance the image of the prostate. I can tell you that it was very uncomfortable to say the least.

After attending the Man to Man support group meeting I walked away with the determination that I would not follow any radiation therapy or a radical prostatectomy, because after talking to some of these men and seeing some of the results and after-effects of these procedures I felt they were not for me.

I try to attend the support group meetings every month unless I am out of state. I attend the meetings for the feedback that you get from the various men, also the fact that some men can benefit from what I have done. I think a lot of them could benefit from my experience and treatment or protocol. In addition, our group has the capability of getting news from the "world wide web," which is a huge computer data base, as to the latest treatments and latest discoveries which is very important.

Man to Man to me is a very positive support group. After having a meeting with one of my doctors out of town, I had come back for one of our group meetings, I told you, Dennis, and all the men present that I had gotten more information at one of our meetings than if I had talked to two hundred doctors. I still say that today.

That is a true statement, because at the first and second support group meetings I attended, as the men were all introducing themselves, and stating their conditions there was more data available there then in most doctors offices.

I will certainly continue my association with our support group and as far as my family is concerned their reaction to the support group is very positive and favorable. My wife also attends the Side by Side group meetings. She feels that every bit of information you can get is helpful no matter what it is.

The information we all get at the meetings, our own searching and reading actually gives you a leg up on the urologists and the oncologists that we see; they seem to lag and be far behind in using some of these latest techniques. For instance, Dennis had mentioned to me the PSA 2 (prostate specific antigen type 2 assay; reports the percentage of free-PSA to total-PSA). This test can be helpful for screening purposes. Also, we have all talked about the PSA RT-PCR (PSA reverse transcriptase-polymerase chain reaction) which is another blood test to show if micrometastatic cells are circulating in the blood stream. It may be useful as a screening tool to help avoid unnecessary invasive treatments. (RT-PCR is not available as of early 1997, the company has pulled this test off of the market). These tests have been available for over two years and there is sufficient data from various experiments that shows that these tests are very beneficial. Our doctors in this area are only coming around now and starting to use them.

The intermittent hormonal therapy that I am on has been around for about two years and the doctors here are just starting to realize that this form of therapy may be a viable treatment to use. I think if you depend on your doctor, your going to end up doing what he tells you to do without any input from yourself in choosing a treatment option.

Your first line of defense is to join a support group immediately after diagnosis like I did. It took me only two days to do this. I can tell you that after I joined the group and went back to the doctor with all the information I had obtained, I felt extremely confident. Anything I said to the doctor or proposed to him I knew, that based on the groups information and fact, that I could stand up to him and not bend to his will. This worked out very well for me. And of course I was very tactful and diplomatic. The doctor has not balked at this knowledge I have and everything has worked out fine for me.

The local doctors in my opinion do not read up on the experiments that have been done with the CHT alone as a treatment for PCa. That is why they don't like to use it. But through our group and my own research, I found out about how successful this sort of therapy could be in treating my PCa and I chose it.

In my opinion it is important to use hormonal therapy early in the game and the doctors have been trained by papers and studies written a half a dozen years ago which recommend the hormonal therapy after you go into a stage C or D prostate cancer. (Stage C, is a tumor clinically localized to the prostate area, but extending through the prostatic capsule, and may involve the seminal vesicles. Stage D, is metastatic or spread of disease, when the horse is out of the barn so to speak). The most effective method in my opinion is to use the CHT early, then if you must have other protocols such as surgery, radiation, seed implants, or cryosurgery, your chances of success are much greater.

The information out now is if you do use CHT before any one of these procedures you prevent the cancer from spreading outside the margins significantly and increase your chances, by a great percentage, that cancer cells will not escape the prostate.

I have been on Lupron and Eulexin known as CHT from the beginning. I did switch to Casodex because it is more convenient for me to take one pill a day as opposed to six pills a day. I learned about Casodex at our meetings. We knew about this before the doctors or the pharmacists did. I read about many studies done in California and Canada regarding intermittent hormonal therapy, or pulse therapy, keeping the PSA down and extending the life of the CHT. That is why I chose to do it. I also read some research papers that the CHT can kill cancer cells, in about 10 percent of PCa patients.

If my PSA rises, I can start it again, and in the back of my mind I have an out. Mine is cryotherapy or cryosurgery (the use of liquid nitrogen probes to freeze a particular organ to extremely low temperatures to kill the tissue, including any cancerous tissues). Even though the FDA (Food and Drug Administration) calls this experimental, it sounds pretty good to me. The doctors are pretty good with this procedure now especially with the three dimensional transurethral ultra sound guided procedure.

I have done a lot of thinking about at what number I would start the CHT if my PSA starts to rise, the doctor suggests that I start at 8.8 my original number, but I think that I may start sooner.

While I was in California I went to the University of California medical center just to see if the doctors agreed with what I was doing. I picked up some additional information on alternative treatments, such as soy products and vitamin supplements. They really seem to be pushing hard in California for a low fat diet and using soy products. It seems that soy has some cancer fighting agents in it. And red meat, they feel, can contribute to cancer.

Those conclusions came from studies done in countries where it was found that low fat and less red meat diets produced a lot less PCa and Breast Cancer. I am on a super anti oxidant supplement program to boost my immune system including green tea, soy milk, maitake mushroom, pycnogenol and Essiac teas.

In summary, I feel very lucky, getting the information that I did from our Man to Man support group, and from the PAACT group in making my own choice (with my doctors input of course), for treatment. Because of this I feel I am in complete control of my treatment and my doctor will be merely confirming or agreeing on what we are going to do. If I step out of bounds and they mention something I never heard of then I might step back a bit and do some rethinking, but so far my doctor has not. I have been up to date on the information as well as they have and in fact at my July meeting with the oncologist, he told me that I knew what I was doing, and I knew as much as he did about it. (Kidding of course).

—JK

Update

Six months after starting intermittent hormonal therapy, my PSA level has risen form 0.48 to 3.3. My urologist suggested restaging to see what is happening. This consists of a Bone scan, CAT scan, and a new biopsy.

This sounded too intrusive to me. I opted to try the new ProstaScint test, recently approved by the FDA. This test injects a monoclonal antibody into the bloodstream.

Attached to the antibody is a molecular particle of Indium which is radioactive. The antibody has an affinity for cancer cells and attaches to them wherever they are in the body. A radio active scanner is then used to scan the entire body and pick up a glow from the cancer cells, wherever they are. This picture, (taken in slices per CAT scan technique), is digitally processed and produces 3D color pictures showing localized prostate cancer and or metastasized PCa. This test should be as good as a new restaging and a lot more comfortable.

Some latest info regarding ProstaScint, (9-97) a physician at M.D. Anderson Hospital, has suggested that this scanning technique has a resolution sensitivity of only about 1cm! Definitely not a tool for detecting microscopic presence of cancer. —JK

Interview 6

My age at present is 57 years old and my major problem, which led me to believe that there was something wrong, was frequent urination. I was having problems during intercourse. There was a lot of pain and burning during ejaculation. Let me tell you this was terrible.

Maybe 3 or 4 years before the pain began I was experiencing a lot of pain in one of my testicles. I went to the doctor and he said it was some sort of blockage in the sperm duct. He didn't say anything else. The doctor was a urologist. A sonogram was done and it concurred with the doctors prognosis of a blocked sperm duct. At that time there was no blood in the urine or semen.

I continued to have the burning and pain symptoms until my wife M finally made a appointment with my regular MD. M did this because if it were up to me I would have never gone. The burning and pain continued for about 3 or 4 months prior to seeing the MD.

The MD did his exam and at the end he mentioned my prostate was quite enlarged for my age but he would continue to monitor the situation. He suggested that I have a Prostate Specific Antigen (PSA) blood test which was a fairly new procedure. This blood test would test for prostate cancer. His words were "I really don't think you have anything to worry about." I was 52 years old at the time.

About a week later I got a call from the doctor; he wanted to see me. My immediate thought was this is not good news. Doctors usually don't call and ask to see you. This call was right after the PSA blood test.

My wife and I went to the MD's office and he told me that he wanted me to see a urologist because the PSA reading had come back quite high, 20. At that time I did not even know what the PSA meant or what it was all about.

I made an appointment with a urologist. He said "we should not be too concerned with the results of the PSA. The fact that my prostate was so enlarged, the DRE my MD had performed stimulated the prostate. All of these conditions could have caused a false positive. I should have another PSA done." This sounded good to me, so I agreed.

A week or so later I got the results of the second PSA, it was higher yet, 50. The doctor now suggested a biopsy of the prostate.

At this point I was starting to get quite concerned and thinking that if this is cancer that's it. I am 52 years old and I am going to die. I was still trying to think positive telling myself this biopsy was going to be negative, that all would be well, trying to think it away.

The biopsy was done at the urologists office. I didn't know what to expect, it was a very painful procedure for me. The doctor went through the rectum. It was ultra sound guided and the whole procedure could be seen on the monitor. This procedure allows the doctor and the nurse visual guidance, as to what area of the prostate to take samples. I did not watch it because, I was not told about the monitor.

I felt the snapping sensations when they took tissue samples of the prostate. It felt like rubber bands going off inside me every time they took a sample. I don't know how many samples they took.

I seemed to be bleeding a lot after the biopsy. I had to clean up in the bathroom at the office. I was given a couple of pills for infection, and sent on my way. I was told to go home, take hot baths, rest for a day or so. I did listen to these instructions and rested for two days. This was hard to do because we own and operate a farm and business has to go on no matter what.

About three days later the doctors office called and told to me come in. I knew this was not great news I was going to get from the urologist. The urologist talked to my wife and I. He said, "the biopsy was positive, you do have cancer of the prostate and the next thing you have to do is a Bone scan, chest X-ray and CAT scan of your vital organs." I asked why these tests have to be done? His answer, "to find out if the cancer has spread or not."

All the tests were done and we had another appointment with the urologist. I always had my wife with me. It is a good idea to take someone with you because when you are told you have cancer you are in shock and don't always hear what the doctor is saying. The other person picks up the parts of the conversation you miss. I know some people who take tape recorders with them to their doctors consultation, some doctors approve, others want to throw you and the tape recorder out of their offices.

The urologist told us "the tumor was not well defined" (not slow growing but a rapid growing tumor). He never mentioned the Gleason Score or anything else as he just wanted us to see an oncologist.

I was really scared now. Words like oncologist and radiation oncologist (a physician who has received special training regarding the treatment of cancers with different types of radiation) and metastasize (spread of disease) were being thrown at my wife and I from every angle. We did not know what to think!

We made an appointment with the oncologist. He gave me a DRE, looked at my pathology reports, slides from the biopsy, all my reports. Then he told me he wanted me to see a radiation oncologist. Another new term for my wife and I to try and understand. At this time I still did not know if the cancer was already out of the prostate capsule and spreading. None of the physicians had given me any information yet regarding my condition.

We made the appointment with the radiation oncologist. He also gave me a DRE during the visit. I remember this very well, because after the DRE he immediately left the room; I said to myself what the heck is going on here? He finally came back into the room, telling me to go back to the oncologist. At this point I was really besides myself, getting more frightened by each one of these examinations by the doctors, nobody telling me anything.

We went back to the oncologist, he told me, that the radiation doctor had called him, to let him know "I was not a candidate for radiation, that he suggested I have a repeat biopsy" the oncologist agreed. I was still in the dark and nobody was telling me what the heck was happening.

The oncologist's reasoning for a repeat biopsy was that both he and the radiation oncologist saw something on one of the tests to indicate that there might be involvement of the cancer in the Lymph Nodes, (see glossary) with something that appears to be a tumor, but he was not sure.

I really did not want to go through another biopsy and told him so. We just left his office and walked out. The next day the oncologist called me, to tell me, there was really no sense in me having radiation or going back to the urologist and having him cut my belly open and sew me back up, because the cancer might have spread. Go have the biopsy, then we can make a better judgement as to what sort of treatment you should have.

I agreed and went for another biopsy, it was a needle biopsy. This one was done differently. I had to lie on my stomach and the needle was placed in my buttock. It took them a long time to set this particular biopsy up. The oncologist had to use sort of a guide, shaped like a BB. Then he drew a circle around it, gave me medicine for the pain. The doctor told me the first shot would hurt a lot, the second needle would be really deep, but I would not feel it. The actual biopsy would be done through this second needle.

I am laying there and the doctor tells me "do not move no matter what" and man I am really nervous now. He was right, I can still remember the first needle, it really hurt and burned. The second needle must of hit a nerve because my legs started to jump. The doctor said "whoops we got to move the needle" he did and then it was not bad at all.

This second biopsy took about 45 minutes. It felt just like the first one in regards to the snapping feelings when the tissue samples were being taken of my prostate. When the procedure was over, I returned home, waiting for the phone call from the doctor.

Several days went by and the doctors office finally called and told me to come in. Let me tell you at this point of the interview, I was and still am very satisfied with my treatment and really can't say any negative things about the doctors who saw me. I really have no big complaints like a lot of other men do. Maybe one thing, they could have done better was to give me a blow by blow explanation of what was going on. Who knows, maybe that was a blessing in disguise.

So off we go to the doctors office for the news. The doctor tells us "the cancer is outside the prostate and is in the lymph nodes. It is a very poorly differentiated tumor and is a very aggressive cancer."

My wife M and I now felt it was the end, that I was a goner. The oncologist stated, "I talked it over with the urologist who did the first biopsy and also with the radiation oncologist. We all feel that you should go on the Combined Hormonal Therapy (CHT). I will start you out with two months of Flutamide (two capsules every eight hours) and then put you on Lupron (injection once a month) combined with the Flutamide." He then asked me if I would like to have a second opinion. He thought I really deserved a second opinion, although the three doctors involved in my case all agreed on what course of treatment would be best for my present situation. He suggested that maybe I would like to see someone out of the area.

The doctor recommended a hospital in New York City, Mt. Sinai and gave me the name of the head of urology there. I made an appointment and went down to this hospital and saw the doctor. We had brought all my slides, X- rays and reports. He examined me and we talked. He agreed with the other doctors that I should go on CHT. The cancer is out of the prostate, into the lymph nodes. The doctor in the city also told me the CHT was quite new but he had men on this treatment for 5 or 6 years and some of them were worse off then I was.

My wife and I felt good about this. The New York doctor had finally given us the ray of hope we needed. We both started to feel a little bit better about my outlook and the future. He also told us " that it was not the end of the world for me and that these drugs (hormones) are really effective."

I started the pills Flutamide first, but only 3 a day instead of the usual 2 pills 3 times a day. This was sometime in March of 1991.

MY PSA prior to the CHT, was 70 and after three months my PSA came down a lot. After 6 months my PSA was down to below

0 this was achieved on CHT. I have been on CHT for over 5 years and have tolerated it very well.

I started to read a lot of books about prostate cancer to learn more about my condition. I learned about the Man to Man support group by seeing an article in the local newspaper. I called the local American Cancer Society, they told where and when it meets. I told myself that this is something for me and I think I would like to be a part of it.

I attend the meetings regularly because I want to keep up with new information that is coming out. I like to talk to the other guys who are on the same type of treatment, to see how they are doing and to see if they are doing anything else to fight the cancer. I just think it helps to keep in touch with the latest news about prostate cancer. Our support group provides me and all the other men in it with this news.

After attending the meetings for about three years now and looking back I feel that I was one of the lucky ones who got good information and a good course of treatment from the doctors in the community. I really had no other choice for treatment.

As far as trying the intermittent hormonal therapy (pulse therapy) until your PSA starts to rise again. This rise in PSA may or may not happen. The reasoning behind this stopping and starting theory is to prolong the life of the CHT treatments. I really haven't considered this yet, or thought about it much for me. I know that several of the men in our support group are trying it and having good results so far.

The cancer still scares me especially when I get aches and pains; it makes you think the cancer is back. But as we all know every pain you get is not cancer related. When I got Lyme disease (a painful joint and neurological disease transmitted to humans by the deer tick) I was hurting so much all over, I thought the prostate cancer was back. You know Dennis, we have both had prostate cancer and Lyme disease. The Lyme mimicked cancer in some ways with the joint pain that I had and all the symptoms you had; we both thought it was the big "C" coming back.

When I called the oncologist about all the joint pain, he checked me over for cancer and said all was OK. I asked him for Lyme blood test due to the fact that I do own a farm and am always outdoors. We do live in a very highly infested area that has the Lyme ticks. Dutchess County is number one in the nation for Lyme disease.

The oncologist did two blood tests for Lyme disease on me and both came back negative. I was getting sicker every day. One morning I could not get out of bed. I really got scared that the cancer was back and I was now going to be a cripple. I was real tired, could not and did not want to do anything. I finally found an out of town doctor who treated me for Lyme even without the positive blood test. He put me on heavy doses of antibiotics. I am feeling much better now. Dennis you know exactly how it is, because you went through the same thing and as a matter of fact we both go to the same Lyme doctor. It took me over four months to feel better and I know it's taken you much longer.

The support group is great and we do get a lot of the latest information on prostate cancer, but not just on cancer. I remember at one meeting we had as our guest speaker, an expert on Lyme disease. You had invited her because you felt it was important for us to know about Lyme disease, because it attacks our immune systems. We who have or had cancer must keep our immune systems operating at full speed.

Another guest speaker was a Chiropractor, who discussed nutrition and cancer; she was very interesting.

The only thing negative about our support group is that it has gotten so big we don't know each other's names anymore. I miss that feeling of knowing each other. I know you are trying to fix that some how. Also there are a couple of guys who try to dominate the meeting, but you are also working on that problem.

I will continue to go to the meetings and my wife likes the Side by Side very much. I don't like mixed meetings, but I do like it when the women join us when we have a guest speaker. It works out well. Our support group has helped my wife M and I cope much better with the prostate cancer.

As far as the two I's incontinence and impotence, I have never had a problem with incontinence. With impotence, I must say that I do have a problem, but at times there is sex without using any devices such as the pump or the injections. Sex does not hurt anymore, of course there is no semen just like the aftereffects of the surgery (radical prostatectomy). I have changed my diet around to low fat with less red meat and I do take some vitamin supplements, including a lot of vitamin C.   —DS

Update on DS 12/97 After over 5 years on CHT, I have decided to start the intermittent hormonal therapy. My doctor was very reluctant to do this but I have insisted and he has agreed. The doctor feels if it is still working why change. My first PSA is due in December of 1997. I started the intermittent 4 months ago the end of Aug. I had a Testosterone level check and it was 40. Very low so even though I am off the CHT it still appears to be working. My decision to start Intermittent Therapy was based on what I learned at our support group meetings and how the other men are doing who also started it. *(PSA 1/9/98 <0.2 good news)*

Interview 7

My name is LB and I am 79 years old. I have been living with prostate cancer for over 5 years now. My initial symptoms were frequent urination. You know, getting up at night quite a number of times to urinate with extreme urgency; I could not hold my urine and I had to get to a toilet real quick or I would wet myself. I also felt some internal irritation, which was painful ejaculation and painful urination. These symptoms got me to a doctor.

I was working at that time for a very large corporation, over 18 years and had been going for a physical every once in awhile sponsored by the company. This time because of the symptoms I had been experiencing I decided to go see a urologist and he gave me a checkup consisting of a Digital Rectal Exam (DRE) and a blood test called the Prostate Specific Antigen (PSA). The urologist told me "I had a very enlarged prostate."

Several days later the doctors office called me with the results of the PSA and it was over 80. Considering the normal range of 4 this was very elevated and the urologist suggested a biopsy be done.

The biopsy was done in 1991, exactly when I do not remember. My age at that time was 74. The actual biopsy was done in the hospital, it took about one hour. It was considered same day surgery. I did not find the biopsy procedure very uncomfortable at all.

The biopsy showed a malignancy of the prostate. The urologist suggested a Bone scan and some other tests be done in order to see if the cancer had spread to any other organs or parts of my body.

Several weeks later in the doctors office he told me I had prostate cancer and that it was already out of the prostate capsule. He had reached this decision based on the results of the Bone scan, CAT scan, and the Ultra sound of the prostate.

The urologist immediately recommended a series of radiation treatments because the cancer had spread out of the prostate capsule. He suggested a radiation oncologist.

I fully accepted this recommendation and saw the radiation oncologist. He concurred with the oncologist's opinion. The treatments were started at Vassar Brothers Hospital here in Poughkeepsie, N.Y.

There were a total of 37 treatments in all; it was a very bad experience for me. After the first few treatments I became very ill. I had to call the radiation oncologist and cancel my next appointment. I could not move because an area in my groin was very painful. One particular night I thought I was really going to die. My insides were on fire and when I told the radiation doctor this he told me he did not know why I was so sick and he also told me, "I worry too much." Of course I worry after all it is my body! Anyway several days later I resumed the treatments. They were the kind given with the linear accelerator machine, supposedly the latest technology out.

I could not work because I was so sick. I could not even drive; the American Cancer Society (ACS) provided me with drivers who took me back and forth for my radiation treatment. Throughout the entire ordeal, transportation was, a free no charge service from the ACS. I cannot give them and their volunteer driver program enough credit and would like to now officially thank them.

The side effects of the radiation treatments were awful for me. I had a catheter (a hollow flexible tube which can be used to drain fluids) in my penis for the urine for a very long time, over eight weeks. I even got the radiation treatments with the catheter in me. The people doing the treatments said that this was alright to do.

I never got married and am a bachelor. To take care of myself in the beginning of the radiation treatments was very rough. I could not even go out to buy food. Volunteer drivers for the Meals on Wheels foundation brought me my meals. A reasonable fee for the food was charged. This also is a great service and I would like to thank them too. I even had to bother one of my neighbors, an elderly lady, who helped with some meals.

I became an emotional basket case. I started to fall apart from fear of the cancer and the aftereffects of the radiation. I sought the help of a social worker at the hospital and she suggested that I go seek out a support group held at the ACS, called The Patient Support Group. They were all women, I did not feel very comfortable at these meetings.

Then one day you, (Dennis O'Hara) walked into the meeting and we met. You spoke to me about prostate cancer. You were the first man to talk to me about it. When you told me that you were going to form a prostate cancer support group, well that was music to my ears. That was in May of 1993.

So Dennis O'Hara and I became good friends and when our support group started I attended the first meeting. This was in July of 1993 and I haven't missed many since. I remember being very excited about it. I was going to meet and talk with men who were in the same boat as I was. Now I consider myself a charter member.

I attend the meetings because of all the information that is given out. We are on the cutting edges of most new therapies that are being used to fight PCa. I want to be around for a while. The group and you give me the incentive to keep going on, not to give up.

You and your family have become my good friends. Besides this I must attend all the meetings because I am in charge of keeping the attendance records, which is a pretty important job. The ACS needs to keep a record of the number of men we have at each meeting. We also have to keep all their names and addresses so we can put each new man on our mailing list to keep them informed, even if they don't come to the meetings.

The support group has also had some very interesting speakers, such as an oncologist, a urologist, and a radiologist. I would never have been able to question and learn from these doctors what I did if the support group was not in existence. There is a tremendous feeling of comradeship and a feeling for each other because we are all in the same boat.

I am a very quiet person and don't do much talking, but at the meetings I take it all in. If someone asks me a question about PCa I can give them an educated answer from all the information I have gained through our support group.

There really is not anything negative that I can see about our support group. There is no money involved or dues, it is absolutely free and it is a good arrangement all the way around.

I will continue my connection with our Man to Man support group so I can be better informed about my condition. You see the doctors don't tell you enough about your condition, but the support group does.

My present treatment is the injection of Lupron once a month and a daily pill called Casodex . This therapy is called the Combined Hormonal Therapy (CHT). What the CHT does is basically block the testosterone which is made by the testicles. This testosterone feeds the cancer. The CHT also chemically castrates you just like you would have had a orchiectomy (the surgical removal of the testicles). I am now aware of a Lupron injection which lasts for 3 months.

This CHT treatment was started because two and a half years after radiation, my PSA started to rise. The radiation had failed. I don't know how high it went, but as of this writing it is now less then 0.1.

Looking back on it now and knowing what I know from attending our support group meetings, I probably would have gone on CHT first. The radiation was real bad for me with lasting side effects. It has been over five years since radiation was completed, I am still very uncomfortable with bowel urgency and some fecal incontinence (bowel movements). My rectum is still burning.

I seem to be tolerating CHT pretty good although, I am now impotent and have hot flashes. I switched to Casodex because of less side effects and you only have to take one pill a day as compared to 6 pills a day with the Eulexin. It is a lot easier now to remember only to take one pill a day besides my other medications.

I would like to thank you, Dennis O'Hara for starting the Man to Man support group and helping to change my whole physical and mental attitude and giving me a great improvement on life in general. I strongly urge anyone who is diagnosed with prostate cancer to join a support group right away. You will definitely profit from it healthwise.   —LB

Interview 8

FA had an enlarged prostate for 5 or 6 years. His doctor finally sent him to see a urologist and he was diagnosed with prostate cancer. This was in 1991 and he was 75 years old.

As usual just two options were mentioned: a Radical Prostatectomy, (RP) and Radiation Therapy, (RT).

The urologist wisely recommended against the RP based on the patient's age and the fact that he had a heart condition.

FA then got full external beam radiation therapy consisting of about 35 to 37 treatments. Other than no appetite and diarrhea for a short time, there were no immediate aftereffects.

However, one year later FA started to have severe rectal bleeding. This was about April 1992. He went to a gastroenterologist (related to the digestive system and intestines) for the bleeding and the doctor discovered that his blood count was way down and sent him to the hospital where two pints of blood were given to him.

The gastroenterologist then sent him to Westchester Medical Center, in Valhalla N.Y. for further treatment of his rectal bleeding. At this hospital they did some laser surgical procedures on his rectum and intestines that repaired the damage he sustained from the external beam radiation which was causing him to bleed from the rectum.

While he was there for the rectal bleeding they also discovered he had a bad valve in his heart and they successfully repaired that.

There was no further treatment for the prostate cancer until July of 1993. His PSA was rising and he was put on Combined

Hormonal Therapy (CHT). In October of 1994 his PSA had risen from 3.5 to 4.9. One month later he was taken off Eulexin and his PSA went down. This happens in some cases when one of the CHT drugs are discontinued.

He is presently on the three month injection of Lupron instead of the injection which lasts only one month.

FA is now 80 years old, in pretty good health, his PSA is under control. If his PSA goes up again he will probably be put on Casodex in addition to Lupron. Sometimes this works in lowering a PSA.

Even though FA has done well, if he had it to do over he states, "he would go on CHT for as long as possible instead of immediately having radiation."

FA has attended almost every meeting of our Man to Man support group and he is a charter member so to speak. He started with Dennis and LB in the patient support group meetings with all the women before Dennis started our Man to Man support group. He says he has learned a lot here and enjoyed the good fellowship. He feels every man who has prostate cancer should belong to a support group, if for no other reason than to keep up with the latest events.

This is a good example of a man who did not make any major mistakes and has done well. Of course the fact that he was 75 years old when he was diagnosed helps. FA likes to quote his doctor who says "You have a better chance of being done in by a truck than by prostate cancer."   —FA

Update on FA 1/1/1997

FA has been experiencing some extreme pain in the groin area and has consulted with his oncologist. He has had a Bone scan and a X-ray of the area and it has shown that he has a fracture in his groin plus some hot spots (hot spots are referred to as cancer which has not yet turned into a tumor) in the area of the groin.

His oncologist has recommended treatments of chemo therapy, specifically (Cytoxan), which he has started. After only one treatment, his blood count was too low so his oncologist stopped the chemo and suggested he see a radiation oncologist.

FA did see the radiation oncologist who studied the reports and films and has started a regimen of external beam radiation to help heal the fracture in his groin and to kill, so to speak, the hot spots. There will be a total of 13 treatments.

He has been on Lupron alone and his PSA has been climbing steadily since November of 1995 when it was .5 to 4.8 in November of 1996.

He has discussed with both the oncologist and the radiologist, the possibility of starting back with the total hormonal blockade, which will include an injection of Lupron in addition to the pill Casodex. To date both doctors have not given him an answer, but he is going to press them into agreeing to this.

He has heard enough evidence and has received enough literature from the support group meetings, to feel this is not such a wild request and he also knows that sometimes a PSA can come down by doing this. –FA

Interview 9

JM was a member of our support group since it's inception in July of 1993. He attended all the meetings. Unfortunately he is not with us any more. He was my best friend and I (Jules) will tell you what I know about his story.

JM was a classic example of what he later realized men should not do. He was diagnosed in 1990 at age 72. I don't know the details, but he was a very healthy 72 and always went to a gym to work out and lift weights etc. Because of his health and his stamina the doctor and JM decided on a Radical Prostatectomy (RP). In looking back he felt that this should not have been done. If for no other reason, his age, he was over 70.

But because of his physical vigor and his outlook, his understandable attitude was "what the heck, I am in good shape, let's get rid of the problem." Of course like the rest of us in those days, he had very little information to go on.

The RP was done and in less then one year the cancer came back. JM was put on a full course of radiation, 37 treatments. This didn't help either and his PSA kept going up. He was now experiencing some back pain and cancer of the bone involvement.

He was then put on the Combined Hormonal Therapy (CHT) and his PSA was still climbing. His PSA went to 47. A Bone scan and X-rays showed a tumor on his spine. He was having a hard time getting around and his quality of life was now being affected.

Chemo therapy was started and JM was getting very sick and weak from the chemo. Both Dennis and I (Jules) talked to him on many occasions. He related to us how sorry he was that he had the surgery (RP) and that if only he had known how bad his quality of life was going to be he would have taken his chances and maybe done nothing.

On December 28, 1995 I got a phone call from co-author Dennis. He informed me that JM had passed away that day at a diner as a result of a sudden heart attack.

JM also had a problem being kept informed by his doctors, not an usual situation. Remember everyone is entitled to know all pertinent information including all test results about one's condition and here in New York State it is a law, if you request copies of your results you must be given them. You may be charged a small fee.

One incident stands out in regards to this last statement. JM had gone to Lahey Clinic in Boston for a complete check-up and had brought all his records with him.

There at Lahey they discovered that on his Bone scan there showed some hot spots, not tumors, but a warning signal that should not be ignored. JM had that Bone scan done a year before and no one had ever informed him of these hot spots. They did become tumors and were causing him a lot of pain and discomfort and external beam radiation was done to effectively treat the condition.

This is a classic case of a patient trusting his doctor to read the reports and to convey all information to the patient; this does not always happen in the real world. JM became very angry and upset over this gross mistake, and discussed it with our group and his family. JM did not want to make any waves and possibly make it tougher on the rest of the men in our support group.

Both Dennis and I urged him to get all his records and to compare the last Bone scan and the one done at Lahey and sure enough the hot spot was present a whole year before he was made aware of it.

Dennis went to the Hospital to have the procedure changed; when the scans or X-rays or any other tests are done to detect prostate cancer which has spread, if the hospital could possibly alert the doctor's office by putting some kind of identifying mark on them so as to call attention to a possible serious condition. He was told "it was not the hospitals or the doctors responsibility to notify the patient about reports but that it is the PATIENT'S ULTI-MATE RESPONSIBILITY to find out about their reports."

Looking back: at age 72 JM possibly should have been put on CHT at once. This therapy may very well have lasted for years and JM's quality of life would have been much better.

JM was always happy to share his experiences with the support group. It made him feel better to get everything off of his chest at the Man to Man sessions. Of course he hoped this would be of help to other members.

The one redeeming factor in this whole story is that the poor man went fast and did not have any long periods of suffering.

Finally there had been no evidence of heart problems, but his widow feels that JM may have overdosed on the chemo and that it just wore his heart down. We will never know.   — J.M.

Interview 10

AS is another case where his doctor did not keep him informed and he feels, another example of what not to do. In 1995 at age 66 he had his regular annual physical. Nothing was said and it was assumed everything was OK.

Six months later AS accompanied his wife, to a physical with the same doctor. His wife then asked the doctor for a print-out of all her test results. This gave AS an idea and he asked for a print out of his last exam and results.

It looked good except there was a mark next to his PSA results. It was 5.5 which is a little above the number 4 which is the accepted number for a safe PSA. Actually between 4 and 10 is a grey area. The majority of men with these numbers do not have PCa. The policy here is to wait and then do another PSA after four to six months. If the count is rising, this perhaps calls for a biopsy of the prostate.

Six months later AS had another PSA test. It had gone up just a little. Both his doctor and the urologist thought there was no problem. Then he went to a third doctor at a Veterans Administration hospital. It was there that he was finally given a biopsy and diagnosed with PCa. This was a full year since his annual physical where the PSA test showed up as elevated.

After diagnosis he started coming to our Man to Man support group meetings. He told his story and listened to others, and then he decided to take his time and be very cautious about either surgery or radiation and consider starting on the Combined Hormonal Therapy (CHT).

However, he decided to have the surgery, and even though he had heard many disaster stories about Radical Prostatectomy (RP) from the group and others he continued to go ahead with RP.

Right after the surgery, the urologist told his wife all was well. Unfortunately he had a recurrence. His PSA is rising slowly and eventually he will be put on the CHT.

There is more to this story. During the operation the surgeon accidentally cut him in a crucial area which makes urination difficult. It may be possible to have corrective surgery, but to this day AS does not want it. The result of this accident was a lot of pain for months after the operation. It is over a year since the surgery. He no longer has pain, but because of what happened, he now urinates as a spray.

AS also says he is not incontinent. Yet he lacks confidence and still wears adult diapers just in case. He was left impotent which is a common aftereffect of this type of surgical procedure.

AS was 67 when he had the surgery done. After 70 the surgery is not normally done, and 65 to 70 is a grey area. The renowned Dr. Walsh does not do this operation after age 65.

What if AS had to do it all over? He says he would get a second opinion and definitely not have the surgery. He would get more information and opt for radiation or the seed implants. Another option he might have considered was to start off with CHT, before making any other decisions.

There is a good chance this would have lasted at least two years or more and by that time significant advances have taken place in the treatment of PCa.

AS likes telling his story at our Man to Man support group meetings. He hopes he can be of help to newly diagnosed members. The group can be a real help to someone who has to make a decision, but as this case shows, it is important for the person to have an open mind. —AS

Update on (AS), MAY 1997

Although we do not give medical advice, Dennis and others in the group tried to get AS to take more time, evaluate his situation further before making any final decision. AS had a high gleason score, he was obviously not the best candidate for RP. If he had gone on CHT, there would be no serious aftereffects and he may have been alright for 2 to 5 years. Unfortunately he made the decision and proceeded to have the surgery.

This past year has been very difficult for AS. He has suffered constant pain due to errors made during the surgery mentioned previously.

An oncologist who spoke to our support group mentioned that if cancer is already spreading, RP can actually be a negative and the spread may be accelerated due to the exposure of the cancer to air. This appears to be the case with AS. His PSA has been going up and he was recently diagnosed as having colon cancer.

The above is a worst possible scenario. Men do not normally die directly from PCa, but when the cancer spreads, this is when one's life is in real danger. We hope that others will learn and not make the same mistakes. That is after all the purpose of this book and our Man to Man support group.

Interview 11

GK was diagnosed in 1992 at age 70. A biopsy showed cancer in two lobes of the prostate. He was at stage B (cancer still confined to the prostate) with a gleason score of 5. His PSA was 12.

GK chose external beam radiation to fight his prostate cancer. In all, 35 treatments were given. His PSA is under control now and he has this checked twice a year.

Looking back GK may not have opted for the radiation if he had been told of the possible aftereffects. His main problems have been gastrointestinal. This means cramps and frequent trips to the rest room. He has had some rectal bleeding and some fecal incontinence which is proving to be a big nuisance. Recently the doctor gave him some pills to try and reduce his cramps and reduce his bowel urgency. GK has learned to live with this condition. As far as the rectal bleeding he is considering having the same procedure that FA has had; to have some laser surgery done to the colon and rectum to control the bleeding.

The Man to Man support group has been an important part of his life. He has always attended the meetings regularly. It makes him feel better to tell his story. He feels especially good over the fact that newly diagnosed men can hopefully benefit from his experience.

GK feels that his prostate cancer is under control and that no further medical treatment is needed for it, but he is considering some medical alternative to his other problems. —GK

Interview 12

SA is another man who has belonged to our Man to Man support group since it started in July of 1993.

He was diagnosed in 1989 at the age of 60. He had a warning because of frequent night trips to the bathroom to urinate. He had previously seen two urologists. A cystoscope had been done and showed nothing. During another procedure, called a Transurethral Resection of The Prostate (TURP), some cuttings taken from the prostate were found to be cancerous.

A radical prostatectomy was performed in 1989 at Johns Hopkins Hospital in Baltimore, MD by the famous Dr. Patrick Walsh. This urologist is particularly well known because he pioneered the movement to spare certain nerve endings during this surgery so that potency can hopefully be preserved.

It was soon determined, before SA had left the hospital, that the cancer had already broken out of the capsule. Remember we had mentioned elsewhere how there are billions of cancer cells and some of these cells can escape, but this may not be discovered until after the surgery and is not the fault of the surgeon.

For two years no treatments were given and SA was monitored every six months. Then a rise in PSA took place. It went from 1.4 to 416, in December 1992. In six months he went to stage D2 and the cancer was found to have gone to the bones.

SA was put on Lupron and Flutamide, the Combined Hormonal Therapy (CHT). In six months his PSA dropped dramatically to .8. He found out through our Man to Man support group, that Flutamide can have some bad side effects. Thanks to this knowledge he became aware of possible elevated liver enzymes, which can cause liver damage. He was then taken off Flutamide, and put on Lupron alone. His PSA remained stable for three years.

SA is also impotent and suffers from some incontinence.

Here is the good news on SA: After the first year of CHT he was given another Bone scan. There was almost no sign of any tumor. Apparently he had gone into remission. This is unusual, but nevertheless encouraging. What you hear more often is that after a Bone scan shows any tumors on the spine, radiation is done. This procedure can be effective.

Recently his PSA has risen slightly to 1.7. This is not a high number, but many doctor's feel the fact that the PSA rising is more significant than the number. If a man has a PSA of 50 and it stays there, he has "stabilized" and this is probably alright.

SA now has permission to go on Casodex. He will be on CHT instead of Lupron alone. Hopefully this will control the rising PSA. His PSA as of February 1997, is 0 and he is awaiting the results of a Bone scan.

SA's advice to new cases is you must be your own advocate. Make sure you get all the information that is available. It is your body. If he had it to do over, he would go on the CHT first, then the Cryosurgery or the Seed Implants.

Before our support group was started, SA had sent a letter to a local paper stating the need for a local cancer support group for prostate cancer. Soon after this, in July of 1993, Dennis, did found our group. SA attended the very first meeting and has been an active, enthusiastic member ever since. He has learned a lot by attending our meetings and he has helped many others by relating his own experience. He is the perfect example of an advanced case of prostate cancer who wants to be fully informed. Our Man to Man support group has been perfect in fulfilling this function for him.   —SA

Interview 13

HK was diagnosed in 1992 at the age of 71. There is not much that is unusual about his case and he did not do a lot of the wrong things like some of the others.

During his annual physical it was discovered that he had a PSA of 29. He was sent to a urologist. Ten needle biopsy samples were taken and two were found to have cancer.

He was given the usual option of surgery (recommended against by the doctor because he was over 70), radiation or watchful waiting. The cryosurgery or the seed implants were not mentioned, but when HK brought this up he was told by the doctor "they are too new and have certain unfavorable aftereffects."

Late in 1992 he commenced radiation and his PSA went down to 1.7.

In 1994 his PSA began to rise very slowly to 2.7. He was put on CHT. He had a bad reaction to the Eulexin. Casodex was not in common use at this time. His main problem was severe hot flashes; so he went on the Lupron alone. As of this day his PSA is holding at 0.

HK is being watched. He is now 75 years old, and if his PSA starts to go up, Casodex will probably be added to his treatment.

Does he have any regrets? Yes, even though the urologist had been generally good, complete information was not given out. For this reason he feels he should have gone for a second opinion. He probably would have done things the same anyway.

HK never felt a need for a support group because his morale was always good and he thought of a group as just serving this purpose. However, he saw a notice in the local paper about a Man to Man meeting. He had already made his decisions, but he decided to go figuring he could be of help to others. He attended and did help others.

He was very surprised to discover how much knowledge was discussed at the meetings. He has become a regular. Had he realized how much information was being made available, he would have started attending the meetings much sooner.

As he gets older, and having been afflicted with PCa, HK realizes that eventually we all must die of something. He would rather pass away from something other than prostate cancer. He thinks of dying from cancer as a possible painful death. I think most if not all the support group members feel the same and would rather pass away some day from something else.   —HK

Interview 14

PS was diagnosed in the spring of 1990; PS decided on a Radical Prostatectomy (RP).

A PSA was done 3 months after surgery, it was less then 0.5. The PSA remained at this level for over 2 1/2 years. In the fall of 1992 his PSA began to rise. (This is a typical example of a recurrence after surgery that you hear so little about from the top urologists).

PS was then started on a treatment of external beam radiation in November and December of 1992. This treatment also turned out to be unsuccessful. He now sees an oncologist and was put on an experimental drug treatment that also failed.

Finally PS was put on Combined Hormonal Therapy (CHT). This has brought the PSA back down to 0.5. He does not remember how high the PSA had gone to before CHT was initiated. So far he is doing alright. He knows that eventually the CHT will stop working.

Sometimes a person can be on CHT for a very long time, before it stops working and sometimes CHT stops working in a short amount of time. This is known as Hormone Refractory Prostate Cancer (HRPC).

When this happens it is not the end of the road so to speak and there are many many good trials going on using a number of successful combinations of drugs such as Novantrone (a form of chemo therapy given intravenously) and Prednisone (which is a steroid). This combination seems to work as a pain killer and it also knocks down the PSA and shrinks the tumors.

What is interesting in this particular case is that the recurrence did not happen until 2 1/2 years after the surgery. In most cases when there is a recurrence it becomes known soon after the surgery.

Once a person has gone for 5 years after the RP, his chances are very good that there will be no recurrence. However, no one has a guarantee. —PS

Interview 15

After all the interviews, Dennis and myself will review them to decide which ones go in the book. At first this one looks like a good one to leave out because not much happens. On the other hand, it does pass our two way test: Is it unique? Are there lessons to be learned?

JF was diagnosed in 1992 at the age of 70. During a routine annual physical his PSA was taken and the results were 14.

He was then sent to see a urologist. The urologist performed a biopsy. The pathology report showed that JF had prostate cancer.

JF refused surgery or radiation and did not want any invasive procedures done at all. At age 70, not having surgery was probably a wise decision. He was put on Lupron monthly. Why he was not on the Combined Hormonal Therapy (CHT), including taking the Eulexin no one knows.

There are cases where Lupron alone is taken, but this is almost always because the person suffered a bad reaction from the Eulexin.

JF's PSA has been going up and the last time it was checked it was at 47. The PCa has metastasized to the bones now making him a D 2 stage. One possible step to correct this would be to put him on Casodex. This treatment consists of only taking one pill a day, instead of six pills a day with the Eulexin. With the Casodex there is hardly any side effects and this does help with a lot of people in JF's situation.

His case is different because he was only on Lupron from the start. Also his mental attitude is unique. Whereas most men are shocked to receive the news of having PCa JF was very calm, cool and collected. He went about his business and he did not have much faith in the medical community.

What do we learn here? In most cases too much is done, such as unnecessary surgery. In this case not enough was done.

Obviously the primary physician here leaves a lot to be desired. JF should have gotten a second opinion and he certainly should have been put on CHT.

JF is not enthusiastic about support groups. Not everyone is. He would rather not talk about or think about his PCa. However he did attend one of our support group meetings.

We suggested (we don't tell anyone what to do) that he see an oncologist. He will consider this. He feels it would probably be a waste of time. An oncologist might recommend chemo therapy, something JF will definitely not go for.

He has now applied to become part of a clinical trial at the Westchester Medical Center, with a dietary supplement (called PC Spes) that could possibly help him (more on PC Spes in the chapter "Hope For The Future"). The thrust of the program is diet, holistic, vitamins and herbs. There is no invasive treatment of any kind and this is what appeals to him. JF's attitude has not changed much. There isn't much the doctors can do and he feels "whatever will be will be." —JF

We wish JF good luck.

Update

JF has given up on his doctor and rightfully so. He has put himself in the hands of a doctor who is doing research on PC Spes. This is the herbal supplement which is explained in the chapter "Opinions of Some Top Doctors."

JF has been accepted into this program. He had been on the Lupron alone and his PSA started to go up. The new doctor put him on Casodex also meaning he was then on the Combined Hormonal Therapy. Unfortunately JF's PSA continued to go up and he was taken off of all medication.

It is now August 1997 and JF is 75 years old. He was on the PC Spes from December 1996 to June 1997. Unfortunately his PSA went from 50 to 137. His doctor suggested going off the PC Spes for one month. JF decided to go off it for good.

Meanwhile late in June of 1997, JF started to have a problem with bleeding through his penis and he also suffers from acute urinary retention. JF then went to a leading oncology-radiation group here in Poughkeepsie, N.Y.

The prognosis was that his prostate had enlarged to the extent where one of his kidneys was damaged. A full regimen of 30 radiation treatments was recommended and JF went along with this.

I (Jules) have interviewed the doctor who is doing the radiation. He explained that JF is receiving the treatments in the same area to the prostate, just like anyone who has been given radiation after being diagnosed with PCa.

However, this is a highly unusual situation because JF is an advanced case, (D2) he is receiving lower level doses of radiation.

JF had a catheter installed in June and it must remain in place until radiation treatments are completed. The doctor was very direct with me. The radiation will reduce the size of the prostate and will definitely stop the bleeding. However the doctor does not know if the urinary retention will be corrected.

Obviously the whole purpose of these treatments is not to add to longevity of patient; but rather to improve his quality of life.

Interview 16

Right now my age is 67 years old. I did not have any symptoms to speak of but in late 1992, as a result of a routine physical, a PSA blood test was taken. The result was 6. My internist suggested I see a urologist, which I did.

The urologist spoke to me very briefly and said that the number 6 was just over the margin for the PSA and did not necessarily mean that there was prostate cancer. The DRE showed that I had an enlarged prostate.

About a month later an ultrasound and a biopsy of the prostate were done and the pathology report came back negative for cancer. The urologist told me that I had a case of BPH (Benign

Prostatic Hyperplasia) a non cancerous condition of the prostate that results in the growth of tissues thus enlarging the prostate and obstructing the flow of urine. Mine was a mild case and the urologist told me "to come back in six months, and we will check it again."

About ten months went by and during that time I had another PSA done and it also came back 6. I had another appointment with the urologist. He did a DRE and PSA and told me that he found nothing very unusual and just maybe my prostate was a little more enlarged than the last time, nothing to cause him to be concerned.

Some time later another PSA blood test was done and this one came back a little higher 6.4. Relative to what I had been reading I did not think this was high and was not alarmed. I should have been a bit more concerned at this point because my father had suffered from PCa.

In August of 1994 I went back to the urologist again and now the PSA was up to 7.8. Another DRE check and the doctor said he did not like what he was feeling now and suggested a repeat ultrasound and a repeat biopsy of my prostate. These procedures were done and there were a total of eight core samples taken from my prostate; three of the eight came back positive for cancer.

The gleason score was 3 which the doctor told me, "was a good indication that the cancer was not very aggressive." He also told me that now I would have to do something about it. I had just turned 65 years old.

My next question was what were the chances that the cancer had escaped the prostate and he said, "very low but that we would next have to get an MRI, Bone & CAT scan and a chest X-ray anyway." I agreed with that and all the tests were done.

By the way, I had a rectal MRI where they insert the coil in your rectum to enhance the image of the prostate and I can tell you that it was very, very uncomfortable for me. The technician had a heck of a time getting the coil in my rectum because I was so nervous and my rectum really tightened up; it was very painful. All of the above tests came back negative for the spread of cancer (metastasize).

The end of October 1994, all the results were in and I was left with the decision of what to do about my prostate cancer. My wife and I had done some reading on the subject, and the options that the doctor presented me with were very sketchy.

At this time I found out about the Man to Man support group and attended my first meeting. At that meeting, after telling my story and listening to everyone else's, the combined opinions of all was that I probably should go on the CHT (combined hormonal therapy) because of the type of tumor, my age and the PSA.

Although this seemed reasonable to me, I still felt, and the urologist agreed that I was a reasonably healthy 65 years old and should be able to withstand the surgery. I opted for the surgery. From my educational background I knew something about radiation and that radiation is not something you do lightly, because in some people their bodily tissues react very violently with the radiation. The biggest hazard for me was the thought of incontinence from the surgery, but in radiation you must also consider the possibility of fecal incontinence, (uncontrolled bowel movements) and to me that would be unbearable.

A date for the surgery was made, December 20, 1994. Also I had decided to give my own blood and that was to be done on a weekly basis, for four weeks.

The first pint went OK.! Of course I had to take iron pills to keep the blood count up and that's when my problems started with severe constipation, so I stopped taking the iron supplements. Before each pint you give the technician takes a blood count and if it is too low you don't give any blood. I just barely made the count for the second pint. So I started taking the iron again and the third pint was just barely passable, again my iron count was very low and the fourth pint was never taken because the iron count was too low. It was now a week before surgery. I was also showing a much higher than normal blood pressure all through this period.

During the blood donation, I was spending up to16 hours a day in bed and very tired. I was just miserable and hitting rock bottom. I woke up at 3 a.m. the morning of December 16, 1994 with a pain in the middle of my breastbone, not very severe but a mild pain, I thought it was an upset stomach so I took some antacid and went back to sleep.

By 10 a.m. I knew I had a problem, and in the afternoon my wife and I went up to the local health center, I told the doctor my symptoms; he immediately called the ambulance and they took me to the hospital. At the hospital the doctors did their tests and I was admitted to intensive care with a very low blood count, very low blood pressure and a suspected heart attack. The cardiologist ordered my own blood be given back to me which stabilized my BP and the heart attack. After ten days in the hospital I was released, but with damage to the heart muscle.

The prostate surgery was put on hold. A period of time elapsed, during this time I was trying to build myself up physically to have the prostate surgery. The cardiologist said it was alright with him to have it, so I went back to the urologist for his opinion. His words were "Absolutely not" and I would now have to have the radiation.

I asked the surgeon to talk to the cardiologist, which he did. The surgeon still did not want to operate even though the cardiologist said it was fine with him, if my health improved enough to warrant surgery.

Much debate went on between both doctors and the decision was made that the operation would take place with some early warning devices in place to alert the surgeon to any impending heart problems.

March 21, 1995 was the date of surgery and as far as blood was concerned, it was decided to use blood from the blood bank.

The surgery took about two and one half to three hours and the surgeon told my wife that all went well, with no blood required during the surgery. From recovery, I went to my room and after a while I felt something was wrong; even my daughter remarked that I looked different. After a couple of days, one of the physicians from the medical group I was going to, came in to check on me. They did this on a routine basis, and I remarked to him that I felt as if I was swelling up and could not even get my wedding ring off my finger, and my fingers looked so big. The doctor said it was normal and should begin to improve but he would make the nurses aware of it.

About two hours later I am virtually unable to breathe and gasping for air, the guy in the next bed starts to push his button for the nurse who finally comes in and takes one look at me and starts running up the hall yelling emergency!

Luckily my cardiologist was in the hospital that day and he saw them wheeling me out of my room and into the intensive care unit. Immediately he had them bring me into the X-ray room and did a chest X-ray. He told me that it was not a blood clot but that I was retaining water. My normal weight was 159 lbs. and the next day, after they started to get the water out of me I still weighed 182 lbs.

I was not passing the fluids they were giving me and I think the nursing staff must have lost account of my intake and output and that is how I retained over 20 lbs. of fluid. I went back to intensive care for three days to be dewatered.

I got home and was feeling lousy. The foley catheter (a plastic tube in my penis to remove the urine) is not working! The urine is leaking all the time and I am constantly on the phone with the doctor and he is telling me all is normal.

Three weeks go by and I am having bladder spasms and in a lot of pain. Finally they removed the catheter. The bladder spasms continue, the pain is severe and I am totally incontinent with blood still in my urine. I was bleeding when the catheter was in and I continued to bleed after it was removed.

About a month or so later I was in the yard and realized that I was dry, no urine coming out; two hours go by and I am thinking maybe the incontinence has stopped and I am finally dry. After about 4 or 5 hours of no urine I called the urologist and he told me to go to the emergency room ASAP. The doctor met me at the hospital and tried to insert a catheter into my penis, but he had a rough time doing it because there was a blockage. He finally succeeded in putting the catheter in and told me "we will leave it in for a week and hopefully this will take care of the problem."

The doctor said it was a bladder neck contracture (scarring which can occur at the bladder neck after a RP and which results in narrowing of the passage between the bladder and the urethra). He also said " This is a very common problem during the recovery period after a RP." I since found out that this is not so common.

This was on May 6, 1995. On May 9, I went to the doctor's office and the catheter was removed and then began the circus.

That was catheter number 2 and we will number them because there are a lot more. I had a cystoscopy (the use of a cystoscope to look inside the bladder and the urethra) done to determine the problem on May 12 and left the hospital with catheter #3. It was taken out on May 15. On May 17, I closed up again, now catheter #4 is put in and taken out on May 24. I closed up again on June 9, #5 which was removed on June 12. Another, #6, was inserted on June 13 and removed the next day when another cystoscopy was performed, catheter #7 (from the cystoscopy) was removed on June 16 when the doctor said "I don't know why it keeps closing, everything in there looks wide open" which if so, caused me to wonder why catheter number 7, was needed. My relief only lasted one day and then #8 was put in on June 17th.

By the way Dennis, this is very painful for me to relive this series of events.

This catheter lasted only two days and was removed on the 19th of June. Number 9 was put in on the 27th of June. Then once a week for three Mondays in a row, I went to the doctor and he would run a catheter in and out of my urethra. The doctor said, "Finally I think that you are over this problem." Since we are keeping count that would have been #10,11 and 12.

The doctor did not want me to do any of the pelvic floor muscle strength exercises, because of the continual catheterizing that was going on. The doctor said it was appropriate to start the muscle exercises in September, six months after the surgery. I did them every day but it did not help the incontinence at all.

I decided to consult with another urologist from out of the area by phone and read all my reports to him. He told me that something went wrong during the surgery for the prostate cancer and that he felt that I would never get my urinary problems fixed and I would always be incontinent. I really did not want to hear that but I had to take it under advisement.

I consulted another urologist who advised me to wear a clamp around my penis, and that it would make my life a bit easier. All I had to do was loosen the clamp every hour and then put it back on again. I did try this for a while and it did improve my quality of life a little bit, but I was still basically incontinent.

One of my sons lives in the Baltimore MD area and I asked him to inquire at Johns Hopkins Hospital if anybody could help me in my present situation. He was able to make a connection with a urologist who specialized in incontinence.

I did call Johns Hopkins and talked to the urologist's assistant who made an appointment for me. I went to Johns Hopkins in November of 1995, the doctor tells me basically what the other urologist had told me that I will probably be incontinent and I was and still am, totally impotent. The Johns Hopkins urologist told me to keep doing the exercises even though he didn't think they would help and that he would not do anything for me for at least six more months just in case I was a late bloomer in healing. He also told me that I would more than likely need an artificial sphincter (a mechanical device surgically inserted to control the flow of urine).

Through the winter of 1995-96 and into the spring I used the clamp but I noticed that the urine stream was diminishing in size.

On June 21, I went back to Johns Hopkins, to have a complete uro dynamic testing workup to assess any damage to the urinary system and to see what damage had been done to the urethra. The nurse could not even get the smallest catheter in me and here I was closing up again in the hospital. The doctor had to take over and use the smallest catheter to open the contracture and do a cystoscopy before continuing with the testing. His conclusion, that I had very bad scarring but that my bladder was OK. The doctor and the nurse do the testing and he tells me and my wife, because of extensive amount of scar tissue at and near the bladder neck, the scar tissue tends to contract with time and that is why I was beginning to close again and why my stream was getting weaker and weaker.

The good news however was that the bladder appeared OK and still had sufficient capacity to warrant use of an artificial sphincter. The doctor also recommended a surgical procedure involving small incisions of the scar tissue prior to the installation of the sphincter device to prevent the possibility of future contractures.

After returning home from Baltimore with another catheter, #13 which was removed on June 25, I immediately closed up again and had another inserted #14. This one was removed in early July and on July 4th I had to have another inserted in the emergency room, #15.

After this, the Johns Hopkins urologist agreed to take me on an emergency basis at the end of a day for the surgical procedure. It was completed and required an overnight stay in the hospital. Interestingly, after this surgery, I was totally incontinent but now felt that relief was in sight.

Eight weeks later, the sphincter device was installed **(see picture page 217)** and six weeks after that it was activated. The device works, although I often joke when asked, "Not quite as well as original equipment." One has also to learn to do certain everyday things somewhat differently. A very small price to pay, considering the alternative.

An additional aspect of this journey should be mentioned. Both my wife and I have derived a great deal of knowledge and support as a consequence of our association with the Man to Man and Side by Side groups in our area. With regards to knowledge, the latest technical information about PCa is always available to anyone in addition to basic information that people require when starting on their own journeys. With regard to support, which may be of even greater consequence, one soon realizes that there are many others having the same problems, and by discussion of their problems and solutions we become virtually self supporting.   — JKA

Interview 17

MICHAEL KORDA by Dennis O'Hara
Michael Korda is the Editor and Chief of Simon & Schuster, as well as the author of many best sellers. He had a radical prostatectomy in 1994. He relates this experience in his excellent book "Man to Man".

Michael is a member of our Man to Man group here in Poughkeepsie, N.Y.

I must admit when he attended the meetings, I really did not know who he was. At the time, January 1995, I was still taking care of the attendance and mailings, and when I saw his name I did not make any connection to him being a famous person.

During the meetings he asked many important questions about incontinence and impotence, and about PCa in general. He was then, and still is, just another guy faced with the same problems we all have dealing with PCa.

During several of the meetings, he asked me if we could have a little chat later on. I did not think this was significant, because men are always asking me if we can talk. I always give them my phone number and tell them to call. Such was the case with Michael.

One evening, as I watched a late night TV show, I recognized a familiar face, and said to my wife, "Hey Jackie, I know that guy." Her answer was that I was kidding and who am I to know somebody on a TV show. Lo and behold he starts talking about prostate cancer and mentions that he is writing a book called "Man to Man". A loud bell goes off in my head and I run downstairs to the archives, where my records are kept. I start to look up names on the list and there he is Michael Korda. That is when I discovered he was a famous person.

Anyway, we finally got together and we did have a very nice chat at my home. Michael was very gracious and he was very patient, listening to me babble on as if I was the "Guru" of PCa.

He took some notes and asked questions of Jackie and I. Why had I started the support group, and how I was coming along with my PCa, etc. He put them all in his book "Man to Man" writing many nice things about me and our group.

Our paths have crossed several times at different functions that the American Cancer Society has sponsored. At one of these functions, Michael was a speaker. He has always tipped his hat to me, and shared his spotlight, so to speak. At one function he referred to me as his "mentor" regarding PCa.

In June of 1996 we had a Survivors Day Picnic here in Poughkeepsie and I was asked to be on the committee. My job was to find speakers. I immediately thought of Michael and told the board that I knew somebody famous. They did not take me seriously. I called Michael and asked him if he would speak in June at our picnic since he is a survivor and a local resident.

He immediately agreed. No questions asked, no excuses about being too busy or his schedule preventing him from speaking. Margaret, his lovely wife accompanied him. I believe he even tailored his schedule to appear that day, because immediately after he spoke a car picked him up and whisked him away to the airport. He has given a lot of his time and energy for prostate cancer awareness.

His talk was just great and all the audience, about 500 or so, were all listening very intently to what he was saying. Following the talk, he did a book signing with the proceeds donated to the ACS.

We keep in touch on a regular basis; he always sends me books and PCa related articles. I send him whatever I can find new regarding PCa. He has helped us with some ideas on how to put this book, "Support Group," together.

When Michael's book "Man to Man" was published, Simon and Schuster gave a cocktail party in New York City, to honor him and I was invited. It really was a highlight of my life to attend that party, even though no one knew me, or I them.

Although he has been recognized by many groups and organizations and famous people, I would like to thank Michael now for his unrelenting efforts to make men aware of prostate cancer, for bringing attention to our group, and just for being there for us all. "Thank You".

I am glad I did not have to do an interview with Michael. Can you imagine someone like me who has no literary credits, interviewing Michael Korda. I would have been a nervous wreck, my incontinence would have reappeared right on the spot.

In his own words, "I found an extract from "Man to Man" which will, I think, serve very well, and which says everything I'd want to say."

"IN THE END, my experience with prostate cancer seems to me a hopeful, optimistic one, not so much because I appear to be doing well-though that's gratifying-but because it proves to me that cancer, this particular brand of it anyway, can be overcome, that is doesn't have to be the scary experience, appearing unexpectedly out of the blue, that it was for me. The information is out there, reams of it; new discoveries are being made every day;

there's no mystery about it. The important thing is to know everything you can about the disease, and I'm keeping up on it, from
day to day, relying on friends who send me clippings of the latest
news and advances, and above all on my prostate-cancer support
group, to keep me up-to-date and informed. Nothing could have
prevented my cancer-after all nobody knows what caused it in the
first place-but what a difference it would have made if I'd been as
well-informed as I am now. It happened to me, and I was unpre-
pared for it, totally ignorant.

It can happen to you, too. These days, when I meet a man, I'm
as likely as not to ask him what his PSA is. If he doesn't know, I
urge him to find out. I am still astonished-and appalled-by the
number of men who don't know, or can't remember, or who
haven't been told by their doctors.

There is no reason why 50,000 American men a year should die
from sheer ignorance, or from turning a blind eye to a disease
which is so easily diagnosed at an early stage. Quite simply, the
best cure for prostate cancer is to know as much as you can about
it before it happens to you.

Learning about it the hard way, after you've been diagnosed as
having it, may be the biggest mistake you'll ever make."

From "Man to Man" by Michael Korda

Interview 18

PR was 55 years old when he was diagnosed with prostate cancer.
PR underwent a radical prostatectomy. The urologist mentioned
surgery and radiation. He strongly recommended surgery based
on patient's age. PR immediately agreed. He wanted to be "done
with it."

The ideal situation is: A man is stage A or B. Surgery is successful and no further decisions have to be made. In the case of PR it
is not that simple. Because of a high risk of a recurrence, urologist
wants him to have radiation as a "precaution." Evidently, PR's radical prostatectomy, has transformed him into a stage C.(see glossary)

Now PR is faced with another decision, to have radiation or not.
He is leaning toward not doing this, he has heard about possible

bad reactions from radiation. The question is: Should he be faced with this decision in the first place?

If given the option he could have chosen Brachytherapy. (see glossary) Many radiologists, claim this has been more successful than surgery. It is much less invasive and with just about no after-effects. If the cancer cells have escaped, any procedure would fail. The radical surgery is very invasive and can result in incontinence and impotency among other things. In this case the patient probably should have been put on the combined hormonal therapy (CHT) for a few months.

This is a classic case of a person who was rushed into surgery without having much information. He should have attended at least one Man to Man support group meeting to get some knowledge on the subject of PCa. —PR

Interview 19

CD is unfortunately not with us any more. He joined our support group at its inception in July 1993. He had been diagnosed on March 4, 1992 and could have used a support group then.

His biopsy was done by a new doctor. The previous doctor was aware that CD was having prostate problems and to the family's best knowledge this doctor had done a biopsy in 1989, but no record of a PSA.

When diagnosed, his PSA was 58.6. After that it fluctuated to as high as 183 in November 1992. His PSA stayed below 60 until October 1994, when it climbed to 87. In January 1995 his PSA had gone to 200.

CD was 72 years old when diagnosed with PCa. It should be mentioned that he knew very little concerning PCa. And as mentioned, our Man to Man support group was not yet in existence.

Here is some information on his medical history made available to us by his daughter. In May 1992 he had laparoscopic lymph node surgery and scraping of the prostate at Lahey Clinic in Boston Mass. This was apparently done to gain information. In June 1992 he had 5 weeks of radiation and a CAT scan of his vital organs. In December 1992 he was finally put on CHT. In

November 1993 he had hip replacement surgery and his bones were clear of any cancer at that time.

In June 1994 he got the last injection of Zoladex. He had been switched to this from the Eulexin. Also in June 1994 he was started on chemo, Velban plus Emcyt. In December 1994 doctors at Lahey Clinic recommended Strontium-89. The chemo treatments had ceased, and Strontium could reduce the pain he was having and probably lower his PSA. This was never done because the local doctor objected.

CD's condition continued to decline. In March 1995 he became paralyzed from the legs up to the abdomen. Cancer had spread to the thoracic vertebrae. He was then given cortisone and put on radiation treatments. He continued going down hill. His treatment then consisted mainly of pain reliever's such as morphine. In August 1995 hospice was brought in. CD continued to deteriorate until he passed on later in 1995, on the eve of his 76th birthday.

Two things must be called into question. First, the radiation treatment. Although diagnosis was on March 4th, radiation was not started until June 11th, over 3 months later. Normally surgery or radiation is done within several weeks of diagnosis. Although we do not know his Gleason Score, it was probably high judging by the fast spread of cancer. All indications were that this person was not a good candidate for radiation.

The second factor is the crucial time element. The CHT treatment did not commence until December, thus 9 months passed since diagnosis. During that time period his PSA went from 58.6 to 183 a huge increase of 125!

According to the family apparently a 2 year time period went by between his last known biopsy in 1989 and the PSA in 1992, that resulted in the diagnosis of PCa. The 58.6 PSA at that time would seem to indicate that PCa was present a considerable time before finally being diagnosed.

Thus after a late diagnosis, much more time went by before CHT treatment was finally begun. How much additional time would CD have had if this was not the case? We will never know.

Certain statistics are not available. Such as, how many of the 41,000 men who die each year from PCa, were similar to CD in that they were diagnosed a year or two late. Or they were not effectively treated after diagnosis for a period of months or both these situations? According to the family, CD went to the urologist every 6 months without fail, but that he also must not have known about the PSA blood test, and that's why he did not request one. It is reported that the first urologist CD was examined by, left his practice very abruptly for reasons we cannot mention here, and the family feels this endangered CD's life.

Last but not least, CD had told his daughter that the Man to Man support group was invaluable to him. Although it was too late by then to help with his health problem, he liked the men and his morale was helped considerably.

Speaking for Dennis and myself (Jules) I can say that CD was always cheerful and upbeat. Everyone in the group cared about him. We were all very sad when he passed away, and he will always be in our thoughts.

CD was so well liked in his home town that the local Fire Department has started a scholarship fund in his name and two signs were erected on the main thoroughfare in his honor.
—CD

Interview 20

LF is an African American. He seems to have done everything right and is a good example for others to follow. In September of 1996 LF attended a PCa screening which was sponsored by Vassar Brothers Hospital in Poughkeepsie, N.Y. The screening consisted of a PSA blood test following that a DRE was performed by local urologist. The results of the PSA for LF was 12.7.

He then went to a urologist, was biopsied and diagnosed as having PCa. He was 64 years old when diagnosed. In December of 1996 he was put on CHT-Casodex and Zoladex. Although the urologist gave LF adequate information, he was also ready to proceed promptly with a radical prostatectomy. At first that seemed to make sense to LF. Like so many others he thought: "If there is something bad, why not get rid of it?"

However soon after, LF began to wonder about the possible aftereffects of surgery and he decided it would be a good idea to get more information. He then made a wise decision to go to Memorial Sloan Kettering Cancer Center in New York City for a second opinion.

At Memorial Sloan, he consulted with Dr. Rabin who has had a lot of experience with PCa. LF decided to treat his PCa with a procedure called Brachytherapy. This procedure consists of the placement of radioactive seeds directly into the prostate. Prior to the seed implantation, LF also received external beam radiation, for a period of 28 days. This type of combined treatment is becoming more common. There are less side effects and a shorter recuperating time than a radical prostatectomy.

LF completed treatments on April 17, 1997. So far he has no discomfort. His PSA at last count was 0.4. He will continue the CHT until June 1997, at this time it will be six months on CHT. The prognosis in this case is good.

LF knew of the "Man to Man" support group, he had met Dennis at the screening and was told about our group at that time. "Man to Man" helps out with the registration and answers any questions that the men may have regarding PCa at these screenings.

He attended several meetings where he was very active in asking questions, and gathering all the information he could, so that he could make a wise decision regarding the kind of treatment that would be best for him.

LF has become an advocate for the African American men in our community and speaks to them at his church and other related African American affairs. Urging males in the black community to get screened for PCa, and if they have PCa, early diagnosis and treatment are a must. Black men have a much higher rate of PCa and we explain all of this in the chapter on "African American Men," later on in this book.

He credits the Man to Man support group with helping him over a rough time and allowing him the opportunity to gather important information, and more significant, the chance to speak to many, many men and question them as to the kind of treatments they had and what the outcome was for each person. Sort of a hands on class for PCa.   —LF

SUMMARY OF A FEW OF OUR UNFORTU NATE CASES

A man not put on full CHT for no apparent reason.

A case where a man asked his doctor for test result. Doctor's reply was, "I don't feel like talking about this."

Another case where a man had a Bone scan that showed "hot spots." He was never told this and only found out a year later when he went to an out of state clinic for a complete checkup.

A 77 year old man who may have had a heart attack as result of too much chemo.

A case where a 82 year old man is on radiation. Considering the odds that his quality of life can be adversely affected, this may not be proper treatment for a man this age. Another example of the abuse of senior citizens that often takes place in the treatment of this disease.

A 79 year old mans reply when his doctor told him you worry too much was of course I worry. It is my body and my life. Good answer!

A 54 year old man who has his surgery done at a very prestigious hospital. He is told in medical jargon, not understanding what the surgeon means and assuming all is well, that the cancer had spread to the capsule and probably had escaped. He finds out for sure 8 months later when attending our Man to Man support group meetings he realizes his PSA is becoming unstable. He requests his pathology reports from the hospital, where it states the cancer had broken out of the prostate capsule.

Nine months from time of diagnosis was allowed to pass, before a man was put on CHT. During this time his PSA rose 125 points!

As stated above, knowledge equals survival. In each of these cases, the information gathered at Support Group meetings could have helped these men avoid poor treatment choices and outcomes.

Part 2

DECIDING ON TREATMENT

With hundreds of thousands of men being diagnosed each year, those at an early stage, less than 70 years of age and in otherwise good health will have an important decision to make. Most doctors will omit 3 or 4 options and mention only the RP and the external beam radiation as possible options. Which one of these procedures is best? The answer is we don't know. Years of research involving thousands of men would be required. From what we do know, it seems as though the record of success is about equal.

SURGERY: About half of these men have a recurrence. Now with the more sophisticated PSA and other technical advances hopefully this rate can be brought down. The aftereffects of surgery have been greatly underestimated. Men are told that the incontinence rate is 3%. This may be true under the strict interpretation that a person has no control over their bladder and must wear a diaper. However, a very large number of men do not fall into that category, but must always know where the nearest rest room is because they have to void every hour and frequently at night. Impotency effects a large number of men also following surgery.

RADIATION: Two main categories of people go on to select external beam radiation. One group is the many who suffer a recurrence after surgery. The other group is those who opt for this instead of the surgery.

Also there are some advanced cases, such as D2, where radiation can be effective in reducing the size of a tumor on the bone.

The aftereffects of radiation can be devastating. We mention incontinence from the surgery. This can also occur with radiation, in a few cases. Difficulty or complete shut down in urinating may occur. This can result in long time use of catheters, surgery and a lot of discomfort. Bowel habits can also be affected. Six of our Man to Man members who had radiation all have stomach problems. Three out of the six said they would opt for something else if they had it to do over again.

Many men choose surgery because they feel there is something bad inside of them and they want it removed. Many choose radiation because it is not so invasive as the surgery. Others choose the radiation because of some underlying health reason like a heart condition which would not make them a good candidate for the radical prostatectomy.

A very important factor is age. If a man is in his fifties and appears to be in the early stages of prostate cancer then the radical prostatectomy is a viable choice. Perhaps this also applies to a man in his early sixties. The late sixties is a grey area. Generally speaking it might be best to stay away from the surgery after the age of sixty five.

BEFORE ANY SURGERY OR RADIATION :

1. Get all the information you can. Joining a support group is an excellent idea.

2. Get a second opinion, and copies of all reports and tests.

3. It might be very beneficial for you to discuss with your doctor the concept of at least 3 months of CHT (combined hormonal therapy), this is called Neoadjuvant therapy, prior to any radiation or surgery. The hormones will shrink the tumor and significantly increase your chances that the cancer will not break out of the prostate capsule.

4. Get the newest sophisticated diagnostic tests that are available. (ProstaScint being one).

If you are in the advanced stages of PCa then number 1 is especially important to you.

Cryotherapy and Brachytherapy are in glossary, along with Chemotherapy. Information also appears in Chapters "Cancer in General" and "Doctors Opinions."

CHT (Combined Hormonal Therapy) is in glossary. Almost everyone who has PCa has this treatment at one time or another. This is mentioned many times in the interviews.

BEWARE OF DRUGS

If you were diagnosed with PCa, and especially if you are in the advanced stages, you are probably on some kind of medication. The problem is there are a number of drug combinations that can be harmful. Every year hundreds of thousands of Americans wind up in the hospital because of an adverse reaction to some combination of drugs. Many doctors give out prescriptions without finding out what other medications are being taken by the patient.

A possible back up is the pharmacy. Many drug stores have patient's prescription records in a computer file.

Certain combinations can be dangerous. There are other cases where one medication can neutralize another. We will not mention the various combinations here except if you are on Nizerol, do *NOT* take Hismanal (an antihistamine). Nizerol is often taken for PCa in pill form. This is done after the man refracts (becomes resistant) to the Combined Hormonal Therapy. If it does not work, the next step is usually chemotherapy. This particular combination can result in irregular heartbeat, cardiac arrest or even sudden death!

It was discovered that many drug stores for one reason or another will give this combination out. This all goes back to the fact that you must watch out for your own health and not completely trust anyone. Whether you have cancer or not, these precautions are appropriate: Inform both your doctor and your pharmacy of all medications that you are on. A good idea would be to use only one pharmacy so that your records are all in one place. Make sure your doctor includes on the prescription what the drug is for. This will help the pharmacist give you the correct information. Discard any old drugs. Ask the druggist for the information sheet that comes with each drug. The list of ingredients and certain interactions from other drugs are listed here. Of course you should also read all the information on the container and carefully follow these instructions.

You should know the details of your illness. Yet many people who do ask questions of their doctors, know little if anything about the medications they are taking.

Pharmacists are usually very cooperative. Come right out and ask just what the drug is supposed to do and any other questions you may have. Many times your pharmacist will give you more information about this or your ailment than your doctor who may be too busy.

Finally, it's true that between the doctor and the druggist you should not be put on any bad combination of medication. There are over 2 billion prescriptions filled each year in this country. You can be assured that human error and neglect come into play. A recent U.S. News & World Report discovered that a number of pharmacies, for example, did dispense the dangerous combination mentioned above of Nizerol and Hismanal. If the error is made, it is the consumer who must pay the price. *BE AWARE*! Keep informed on all drugs you take and make sure there are no potentially harmful combinations.

CANCER IN GENERAL

There are a lot of different kinds of cancer. Some things pertain to all of them such as the search for a cancer cure. Many times the hoped for cure is planned to be particularly effective against just certain types of cancer.

We must be careful when generalizing. For example there are books pointing out various disadvantages of chemotherapy without distinguishing among different kinds of cancer. They claim chemo is toxic which is true. They say it destroys the immune system. For 7 to 10 days after chemotherapy the blood count is way down and the person is highly susceptible to various infections, due to the fact that your immune system is being challenged. There is also a possibility that chemotherapy can cause additional types of cancer. There are no statistics on this claim. Some of these books even go so far as to say that chemo has no redeeming value and no one should be given this treatment.

Now it becomes important to separate the different kinds of cancer. We think to say no chemo treatment for anyone is too drastic. Right here in Poughkeepsie, N.Y. we know of a young woman in her twenties who was given chemotherapy treatment by a local well known oncologist. She was treated for non hodgkin's lymphoma. To the best of our knowledge she is now in remission and will hopefully be alright. On the other hand we know of a man who was in his fifties, with the same disease. After a few months of the chemo his immune system had broken down and he died of pneumonia. When it comes to PCa, chemo has been used in a very limited way, and without any resounding success. However the use of chemotherapy has been increasing recently especially now that the drug Taxol is being used in some hospitals to treat PCa.

In making drastic statements that no one should have chemotherapy, it should be kept in mind that this is often a last resort with little other alternatives except holistic.

There is a lot of similarity between prostate cancer and breast cancer. It is not uncommon for certain types of chemo to be used for more than one type of cancer.

Most holistic treatment-herbs, vitamins, diet, etc. are supposed to be helpful in aiding the immune system against any type of cancer.

As far as a cure, not yet. However, there has been more progress with some kinds of cancer than others. For example 30 years ago a child with leukemia was almost certain to die. Today a large percentage of these children survive.

Some chemotherapy treatments can cause heart damage. If you have PCa, the simplest treatment, *Emcyt plus Velban*, can cause heart damage. Some doctors in small towns may not be aware of this. If you are on any kind of chemo, it may be advisable to ask your physician about possibly taking an aspirin or Ecotrin a day as a precaution. Do not take either without consulting your physician because aspirin can be harmful to people with ulcers, or sensitive stomachs.

HOPE FOR THE FUTURE AND ALTERNATIVES

Before getting into the future, let us have a quick look at some options. For early stage prostate cancer A,B, and a few C's, the main options are:

RADICAL PROSTATECTOMY: an operation to remove the entire prostate gland and sometimes the seminal vesicles.

RADIATION THERAPY: the use of X-rays to destroy cancerous cells. Usually 30 or more treatments are required.

CRYOSURGERY: liquid nitrogen is used to freeze and kill the cancer tissues.

BRACHYTHERAPY: this is a form of radiation therapy in which radioactive seeds or pellets are implanted in order to kill the cancer tissue. Although comparatively new and so far used in a limited number of cases, some doctors claim the success rate is higher than surgery. It is certainly much less invasive and much less expensive. This is why Man to Man is trying to have legislation passed in every state whereby doctors would be required to inform each prostate cancer patient on all options available.

Combined Hormonal Therapy (CHT): This is the most widely used treatment for advanced cases where surgery or radiation has failed. Originally, this consisted of an oral pill called Eulexin, and an injection of Lupron. Eulexin was taken 2 at a time, 3 times a day, total of 6 pills. Eulexin has been pretty much replaced by a pill Casodex. Only 1 pill a day is needed and there are fewer aftereffects compared to Eulexin. Lupron is still in widespread use. Administered in one or three month injections in buttocks. Zoladex is a 3 month injection given in stomach.

NEO ADJUVANT THERAPY: It is now becoming common practice to put a man on CHT, 3 to 6 months prior to surgery or radiation. This results in lower PSA and downsizing of the prostate, thus making the surgery or radiation easier, and increasing the chances of a successful outcome. This therapy also greatly increases the percentage of negative margins, meaning the cancer has not reached the edges of the prostate, and possibly escaped into the blood stream. At this point, no cure can be reached. Some doctors prefer to operate at once, the patients prostate may not be enlarged. The surgeon may feel justified not to wait 3 months. Man to Man does not dispense medical advice, but we do feel that having the **neo adjuvant therapy**, is very beneficial in a great majority of cases.

ADVANCED CASES: CHT has been very successful. It lasts an average of 20 months, but in some cases much longer. We have a few men in our support group who have been on CHT for over 5 years and they are still OK. A comparatively new development is intermittent therapy; Some doctors refer to it as pulse therapy. A man who is doing well is taken off CHT for a time. His PSA is watched closely and taken into account. If the PSA starts to rise, the doctor then starts the CHT again. The advantage of this new form of therapy, is to hopefully prolong the time a patient can be on CHT. There are cases where doctors are hesitant to do this. The patient is doing well and why argue with success? Apparently intermittent therapy will be used much more in the future.

Another big change regarding CHT: A few years ago if a man refracted (PSA rising) he was immediately taken off CHT for good. Today this has all changed. Sometimes when a man is taken off Eulexin or Casodex, and just left on Lupron or Zoladex his PSA stays down and he can go along indefinitely like this. We have a number of such cases in our Man to Man group.

Also after a period of time a person who has refracted may be put back on CHT. Every person is different, so the only way to know if CHT will work is to try it. If it doesn't work out, something else can be tried.

RE: A AND B STAGES OF PROSTATE CANCER: Probably not much will change in the future-except that seed implants (brachytherapy) seem to be coming into their own. Two other options being surgery and radiation. For more advanced prostate cancer there is a lot of research going on both with drugs and holistic. Drugs must have approval from the FDA and this could require years of research involving thousands of men. Holistic usually come from the ground, meaning they are natural and grown. They do not require FDA approval. They are usually available by mail order or in health food stores, some herbalists mix their own.

Let me make one thing clear (Jules). There is no sure thing at this time as a cure for cancer. Here is a quote from doctors who are affiliated with a national organization, "PAACT" (Patients Advocates for Advanced Cancer Treatment). "Use of the word cure is totally erroneous. Only when we have discovered the cause of cell mutation from normal to abnormal and how to eliminate it, we will we be able to use the word cure." This is why no matter what kind of cancer a person might have had, he or she is monitored the rest of their lives, just to be sure there is no recurrence at the original site or somewhere else.

Most of the possible treatments listed below do not claim to cure. Some do claim that they can strengthen the immune system.

MUSHROOMS: They have been used for centuries throughout the orient for many health purposes. There are many varieties. We are mentioning here one specific kind Maitake (pronounced my-tah-key). It can be eaten or taken in liquid form. This can supposedly help to regulate blood pressure, blood sugar, insulin secretion, cholesterol and tryglycerides in addition to the ability to support the immune system. It is the latter feature that is important for prostate cancer. A key component called "D fraction" is what sets this apart from the other mushrooms.

1. Many rats with prostate cancer were given Maitake. The result: Not one of these rats developed any tumor on the bone. (LUCKY RATS)

2. An author and researcher named Ralph Moss has written several books on cancer and alternative therapies. He intensely researched more than 100 cancer therapies. The result: He decided the most effective of all are medicinal mushrooms. It is the Maitake which stands out among all the others.

Dr. ROBERT ATKINS: A specialist on diet. He is also interested in cancer therapies. He puts out a monthly newsletter called "Health Revelations" and he operates a clinic called "The Atkins Center" in NYC. He administers the Maitake mushroom itself or the liquid extract known as D fraction. He finds that it inhibits tumor growth in various types of cancer by strengthening the immune system.

NOVANTRONE: A new chemical treatment for advanced prostate cancer. Studies have shown little side effects and that pain and PSA are decreased. The company who manufactures it has applied to the FDA for approval. (approved Nov, 1996)

TAXOL: A possible cancer fighting substance obtained from the inner bark of one of a species of the yew tree Taxus Brevifolia. It's ability to disrupt cell division in humans was first discovered in the late 1960's. Only small amounts of Taxol can be harvested from each tree. Yew trees grow all over, but this particular species grows only in the rain forests of northwestern United States and Canada. This has been approved by FDA for certain kinds of women's cancer. It has not yet been approved (this is Feb. 1998) for prostate cancer. Never the less it is already being used extensively at Memorial Sloan Kettering. I (Jules) am one of those who received this treatment and thank goodness it did improve my condition.

A NEW VACCINE, ANTISENSE TGF-B1: Not yet approved, by FDA, has eradicated tumors in rats and may soon be tested on human brain cancer. Many cancers including prostate secrete a substance called factor-beta which cloaks the cancer cells. This vaccine is designed to alert immune system by preventing tumor cells from making the factor-beta or TGF-B1.

ZOLADEX: Similar to Lupron. Lupron can be injected for one month or in a three month dose. Lupron is administered by injection in the buttock. Zoladex is administered by inserting a long needle into the stomach and it is usually given for three month period only!

Method of application is the main difference between Lupron and Zoladex. With Zoladex an implant is injected which slowly releases the fluid. Some doctors including mine feel this is the most efficient method of delivery.

MARIMASTAT: A new drug by a company in Europe. It is still being researched. It is to be taken orally. This is designed to produce positive results in colorectal, ovarian, pancreatic, and prostate cancer. This is a new method that would effectively inhibit blood flow to tumors and thus block further growth. Even if further tests are successful, this drug may not hit the market until 1999.

ESSIAC: This is one of the better known alternative approaches. This tea is claimed to help many kinds of cancer in addition to prostate cancer. This goes back to 1922 when a nurse in Canada, Rene Caisse, received a recipe from a patient who had gotten it from an old indian tribe in Canada. She started to brew the tea. Herbs are not researched like proposed drugs, so there are no available statistics; however there is a lot of literature out there on the subject of ESSIAC TEA.

Many people, however, who were hopelessly afflicted claim they were helped. The formula consists of cut burdock root, sheep sorrel powdered (includes stem, leaves and seeds) Turkish rhubarb root, powdered and slippery elm bark powdered. You can purchase Essiac Tea from various health food stores. It is possible to obtain this already prepared in a liquid form. Many people who have no illness take this as a health aid to build up the immune system. Not everyone is helped although it is probably true that no harm can result either. At the end of this chapter I will list various herbs that could be harmful. Essiac is not one of them. Also like the other alternative approaches one should continue to take whatever medication he is on. Of course in many cases a person has exhausted all medication before the essiac. Doctors opinions will vary. Some doctors being more open minded toward this type of treatment than others.

MODIFIED CITRUS PECTIN: This is a compound derived from citrus fruits and it prevents the spread of cancer in animal tests. This can be taken as a food stuff without any limitations. It will take many years of clinical trials to conclude that the compound is as effective in human beings as in animals.

It's possible that modified citrus pectin can prevent the metastasis of PCa. Many men with PCa are taking this and there seems to be no side affects.

In recent years, it has been established that special molecules prevent the spreading of cancer in the body. Chains of sugar molecules extracted from modified citrus pectin are particularly well suited for this job.

Many times people who are taking this are also receiving other types of treatment, so it is difficult to measure the effectiveness of modified citrus pectin in these cases. We certainly hope this will prove effective against many types of cancer.

SOY: Is said to suppress the growth of human prostate cancer cells. It contains a substance called BBI which suppresses carcinogenesis. Soy can be taken like milk. It may help women with breast cancer and it may help with PCa. A person can also eat a diet high in soy (tofu products).

SOY MILK: There have been many good reports on this. This is organic soy beverage made from organic soy beans. Some ingredients are fiber, potassium, protein and carbohydrates. This should be taken as a supplement to any medical treatments and this is true of the other holistic such as Maitake mushrooms.

UKRAIN: A plant extract, this is used extensively in Poland to control cancerous tumors. In the United States, Dr. Atkins' health center in NYC, has been working with this. Ukrain is an alkaloid from a plant called celandine. Toxic components need to be eliminated. A scientist from Ukrain developed this method. There are indications that when people with cancer are given Ukrain, their immune system or ability to oppose the spread of cancerous cells improves.

Lab experiments have shown that Ukrain interferes with the multiplication of cancer cells. Unlike chemo this treatment apparently does not harm normal cells. There is hope that this will eventually be delivered directly into tumors. It would then become more effective. Apparently more time will be needed until we know just how effective Ukrain can be.

REGARDING MEDICATION: More time is needed to do research on such things as Marimastat and Taxol. Taxol has been approved for certain kinds of women's cancer but not yet for prostate cancer. Unfortunately research usually takes years.

REGARDING HOLISTIC: Holistic or so called alternatives has always been a grey area. Massive testing involving thousands (which is done on medications before FDA approval) are not done here. What few clinical tests that are done usually involve 10 or 15 people.

There is no agreement in the medical profession regarding alternative treatments. Some doctors are very much into alternatives and encourage their patients to do this along with conventional treatment. Many other doctors, some recognized as top leaders in their fields, are not the least bit interested in holistic or even discussing this.

The American Cancer Society is very wary about alternatives. They feel that under no circumstance should a person abandon medical treatment and depend solely on alternatives. They rightfully recommend to be careful with alternatives. Our local Man to Man support group agrees with this. We have listed in another chapter many herbs that could be harmful.

There are no statistics showing success or failure of alternative treatments. Many people take alternatives along with conventional treatment. The makers of Pc Spes, which is a dietary supplement, suggest in many cases that a PCa patient take their product along with certain chemo treatments. Many others take alternatives when medical options run out.

Late Development: This is a late development in alternative or holistic. Compounds derived from the Chinese Camptotheca tree seem to be active against a number of cancer tumors. The Stehlin Foundation of Houston, Texas announced good results using "9NC" in capsule form to treat pancreatic cancer. If this compound works out, it could be the poor man's answer to expensive chemotherapy. Much more research over a period of time needs to be done.

DR. STANISLAW BURZYNSKI: Has a clinic in Texas. He discovered chemicals called antineoplastons. Chemicals that are found in blood and urine. The doctor claims when taken intravenously through a catheter in the chest, that it can cure cancer. This has never been approved by the FDA. They say there is no evidence that this works and he has been charged with a 75 count indictment. Trial is scheduled to start October, 1996. **(UPDATE MARCH 1997, DR. BURZYNSKI FOUND INNOCENT OF ALL CHARGES)**

Most people who go to this clinic have exhausted all other means. Some claim they have been helped. Others thought they were being helped but had a relapse 6 months or a year later. The evidence is lacking. The doctor argues that he should be allowed to continue the clinic and that patients have the right of choice. It is also true that many people want his clinic to remain open even though there are no guarantees, because they feel this is their last chance.

RESEARCHERS: From MIT, Salk Institute and University of North Carolina have found a protein that allows cancer cells to resist chemotherapy and radiation. That protein is called NF-KB. At MIT they blocked the action of NF-KB. Cancer cells were then killed by TNF. Once the action of NF-KB is blocked, cancer cells can be more easily killed by chemo or radiation. The above is from associated press dated October 31, 1996. We do not know if more testing is needed or when this treatment will actually become available.

New information often comes out like this using either medical terms or letters. As of now we do not know what these letters stand for. Hopefully if this new procedure works out, some time in the future this information will be made available in language that the average person can understand. Assuming there is a bad protein in the body and MIT has nullified or blocked the action of this protein, the news release did not say how MIT accomplished this. What they did say was that by blocking the bad protein they call NF-KB, both chemo and radiation can be administered more effectively. We will have to wait and see.

RESEARCH: Now going on involving over 200 new medicines. There are 48,000 researchers from various pharmaceutical companies. Something new is so-called light-activated drugs. Using a process called photodynamic therapy, they are working on ways to treat cancer by concentrating light-sensitive drugs on cancer cells. By shining a special low power light on these areas, cancer could be destroyed while leaving healthy tissue intact. (The main disadvantage of various chemotherapy treatments now in use is that when successful, it also destroys good tissue). Hopefully this new therapy will one day be used. It would be particularly effective against lung, prostate, brain and stomach cancer.

JANSEN ONCOLOGY: Has come up with a new drug, LIAZAL undergoing tests to meet FDA standards. This drug is a differentia tion agent that acts on both hormone dependent and independent cells. First tests will be with advanced PCa. This drug was first developed in Europe.

Strontium 89 (Metastron): A large majority of patients with advanced PCa, develop bone metastasis. It is still considered prostate cancer not bone cancer, because the cancer originated in the prostate. This can eventually effect mobility as well as cause pain. The main problem usually being pain. Strontium is administered by injection, and it is radioactive.

Strontium 89 has been used extensively. The molecule follows biological pathways of calcium and is incorporated into the bone. This has been very effective for relief of pain. It also increases mobility in most patients. The majority of patients who are given strontium 89 have fewer new lesions, and some have a lower PSA.

HERBAL REMEDIES: Have always been promoted as safe and natural. Most people are aware of possible side affects and dangers of prescription drugs. There are a large number of herbs that contain ingredients that could cause serious toxicity. These remedies are not controlled by FDA or any regulatory agency. The label could be incorrect or there could be improper preparation. Without going into detail, here is a list of herbal remedies that could be harmful: Lobelia, Comfrey, Pennyroyal, Coltsfoot-Sassafras, Senna, Yohimbine, Ephedra, Chan Su (also know as Rock Hard and Love Stone), Tungshueh, Chinese herb balls (marketed under various names), Ginseng, Jin bu huan.

Some of the above can be effective, but because of possible serious aftereffects, you should check with your doctor before taking any of these.

The following have resulted in at least one known death: Pennyroyal, Senna, Yohimbine, Chan Su.

The following can cause very serious damage: Lobelia (if taken in high doses), Ephedra, Tung Shueh, Ginseng, Jin bu huan.

PC SPES: The eight different herbs in each capsule are supposed to have various positive effects on the body.

There have been encouraging results described in the chapter "Doctors Opinions." Also we know that a number of men from the Syracuse NY, Man to Man group have done very well with PC Spes. Their PSA's have gone down dramatically. Many of our Man to Man members here in Poughkeepsie N.Y. have started on PC Spes, but it is still too early to know the results.

It is recommended that a person take 9 capsules per day. However, you can start off with just one or two so your body can adjust to it. Botanic Lab, the producer, does not claim this is a cure. (Nor is anything else a "cure"). But based on limited results so far there is room for optimism that PC Spes will prove to be a big help for those with advanced PCa.

VITAMINS: Alternative doctors are in favor of vitamins. Some medical doctors favor vitamins. Some others while not against, feel it is a waste of money because if you eat the proper foods (which few people do) you will get all the vitamins you need.

Another point we must make here is that most doctors don't know much about nutrition and there is very little time spent on nutrition in medical schools. Perhaps this will change as more and more research is being done on what you eat and how you feel.

There are no bad aftereffects from any vitamin. However, it is possible to overdose on certain vitamins. One should consult a nutritionist or a health food person on proper dosage.

DOCTORS OPINIONS

DR. PAUL SABBATINI:
He is a doctor at Memorial Sloan-Kettering Hospital in New York City. He is a young man who is on the staff of the renowned (oncologist) Howard Scher, who specializes in PCa. I (Jules Schwartz) often wind up talking to one of these associates instead of Dr. Scher. They review each case with Dr. Scher and he is on top of everything. These young doctors are extremely knowledge-able and answer just about all your questions. In my opinion they are better than many doctors who practice on their own.

I asked Dr. Sabbatini his view of the future regarding PCa. He thinks that within a couple of years major advances will be made. He said, "Don't look for a miracle like some drug company coming up with a pill next month that will cure all cases of cancer." Instead he feels the advances will be in stages.

He emphasized the downgrading of the PSA numbers. Whether the count is going up or down or remains the same is the impor-tant thing, and the main benefit of the numbers is that they give us this information. Of course the doctor would like to see every-one with a PSA of zero, but this is not possible.

Many times it is satisfactory if the count remains the same as long as it does not continue to rise. Dr. Scher has a patient with a PSA of 700 who feels good and goes about his daily business. The important thing is his PSA count is not rising, this means that the patient has stabilized.

A word of advise from Doctor Sabbatini: "It is important to keep using the same lab for the PSA testing. A different lab may show a different result." Our Man to Man support group president and my co-author Dennis O'Hara can attest to this, because he had exactly this experience.

We discussed the fact that the news on the latest developments seems to be dominated by holistic with very little going on with medications. However we have mentioned that drug companies alone are engaged in over 200 research projects, so there should be some kind of news soon. Meanwhile many men who have PCa are taking both medication and certain holistic approaches such as soy, mushroom, citrus pectin, Essiac tea etc. In some cases the patient no longer responds to any kind of medication and in this situation no one can blame him for trying certain alternative methods. After all it is his life that is at stake and he has every right to use every possible means to extend it.

Dr. Sabbatini expressed some knowledge about Marimastat. This drug is mentioned in the "Hope for The Future" chapter. This is a new method that would inhibit blood flow to tumors thus blocking any future growth. This is still being tested. The doctor expressed no opinion on this particular treatment, but I'm sure he hopes it will work.

The policy of Sloan-Kettering is to administer treatment to advanced cases like myself (Jules), hoping this will keep the disease under control and as Dr. Sabbatini hopes, the scientists will come up with some real good advances during this time.

DR. GLENN AGOLIATI:
He is an oncologist here in Poughkeepsie, N.Y. Although he has a one doctor practice, he treats a lot of patients with just about every kind of cancer including prostate cancer.

His views on prostate cancer: The emphasis should be on screening and early detection. If a patient is under 70 years old, and shows no signs of the cancer being outside the prostate capsule, a radical prostatectomy may be the choice of treatment. In certain cases radiation may be more appropriate. For example a man may be under 70 years old but have some sort of heart condition. In view of the invasiveness of the surgery, a person's overall health must be taken into account.

Dr. Agoliati is the most compassionate and caring doctor I have ever known, and I have dealt with a lot of doctors. He treated me at one time and still keeps up with my case. He is genuinely concerned with each of his patients, many are in our support group.

Dr. Agoliati is not a holistic doctor, but he does feel there may be something to alternative medicine. This would include things like maitake mushrooms, herbs etc. Also going back to a diet with less meat and fats and exercise. All the above should aid the immune system which he feels is very important. He feels there should be more emphasis on prevention. Some of the above might be good for that too. He points out that although there is no proof of effects of diet, we do know that in a country like Japan where they eat entirely different food there is much less prostate cancer and certain other types of cancer.

Regarding chemotherapy: Dr. Agoliati would obviously not agree with some of the books against chemo, especially the ones that are opposed to any chemo treatment for anyone. We refer to these books in another chapter. As an oncologist, he does administer chemo to many patients who have a wide variety of different types of cancer. He points out that the chemo treatments work better with some types, such as breast cancer, as opposed to other types of cancer. He states that chemo is not a big hit with prostate cancer, but that it is sometimes used for this.

As time goes on there will hopefully be new, improved chemo treatments. Right now Taxol (fully explained in another chapter) is already being administered to prostate cancer patients with some success. At this time it has been approved by the FDA for certain kinds of women's cancer, but not yet approved for prostate cancer.

Dr. Agoliati is wary about making predictions for the future. As mentioned before, he is a very compassionate person. He certainly hopes significant advances will be made soon to treat all forms of cancers.

KERRI WEINGARD:

She is an RN (registered nurse) at Memorial Sloan Kettering who works with Dr. Howard Scher. She may not be a doctor, but she examines many PCa patients and is very knowledgeable on this subject. Even though she is a women, she identifies with and feels bad for the victims of this disease. Kerri points out, for example that over $1.8 billion (annually) have been spent on AIDS research while only about $80 million (annually), a very small pittance, goes for prostate cancer research.

She feels that PCa is much more out in the open now and that hopefully more funds will be made available in the future to help find a cure. She also pointed out that a D stage patient, one whose cancer has spread to the lymph nodes, does not have to become a D2 where the cancer goes further, usually to the bone. Even if this does occur, it is not called bone cancer. It is still called prostate cancer, because it originated in the prostate gland. Kerri Weingard is indeed a dedicated worker against prostate cancer.

DR. HOWARD SCHER:

He is a recognized top specialist in the field of oncology; he deals with advanced prostate cancer and practices at Memorial Sloan Kettering, one of the renowned hospitals for cancer treatment in this country and perhaps the world. He is not as well known as Dr. Patrick Walsh, the urologist-surgeon who has written a book and has appeared on many TV shows. I am very fortunate to be going to this top specialist. Dr. Scher is very optimistic that there will be important advances in the treatment of PCa very soon.

As mentioned before, everyone is different. What works for one man may not work for another. Doctors like Howard Scher have worked with so many men, that there is a better chance they will pick the best treatment for a man's prostate cancer. If something does not work, Dr. Scher has a vast knowledge on whatever else is available. The name of the game is to survive as long as possible, because the medical world is coming up with new treatments constantly.

I (Jules) was going downhill with a PSA shooting up 4 points a month and was given a new life by being treated with the drug Taxol thanks to Dr. Scher. Less than a year ago this treatment was not available. Advanced PCa is a real challenge. Dr Howard Scher is one of those who is meeting this challenge head on. Keep up the good work Dr. Scher!

Personal Comment by Jules: It is now Feb. 1998. Dr. Scher has a staff of many doctors. They have always until now been uninterested in alternatives. Neither Dr. Scher or any of his staff ever said anything negative about alternatives. It was just something that was never discussed.

On my last visit (Nov. 1997) all this changed. They were much more open minded. I was told to eat as little fatty food as possible. They questioned me for the first time on what alternatives I take. I told them maitake mushroom and citrus pectin. Dr. Scher and one associate, highly recommended that I take Soy milk because it contains Genistein.

The big surprise was this: Dr. Scher recently had a meeting with Dr. Sophie Chen, the person who developed PC Spes. I asked him about this meeting. Dr. Scher was very impressed. He asked Dr. Chen to send him various data. Never the less, here is Dr. Scher's exact quote regarding PC Spes, "There might be something to this." This statement coming from an important doctor like Dr. Scher who until recently was not enthusiastic about alternatives, is to me a big deal!

DR.MICHAEL BURKE, DR. DIMITROIS PAPADOPOULOS:
Are top radiation oncologists in a group called Mid-Hudson Valley Radiation Oncology Associates. They are located at Vassar Brothers Hospital here in Poughkeepsie N.Y. All radiology treatment at Vassar Hospital is done by this group. They estimate that at least 15% of those they treat with radiation are prostate cancer patients.

One disadvantage of radiation: With the surgery of the prostate,(radical prostatectomy) they can tell if there is lymph node involvement. If so the surgery is halted. This is not true of radiation. An advantage of the external beam radiation is that it is less invasive than the surgery. Usually surgery is not done after age 70. Some Urologist's do not perform the surgery after age 65. Radiation is often done after the age of 70, although sometimes age is a factor.

In our Man to Man support group, some of those who underwent radiation are doing alright. The doctors said certain side effects, such as rectal bleeding, are to be expected, but usually these things are not serious and are brought under control at least to a point where the person can live with it.

Some other points that the doctors made: The equipment is becoming more sophisticated all the time, meaning less chance of complications as time goes on. They are optimistic about seed implants-(Brachytherapy see glossary) a form of internal radiation, something they are now doing at Vassar Brothers Hospital.

You have heard all along including in this book that you should get a second opinion. Well here is a shocker: Doctor Burke said "each man should talk to two urologists and two radiation oncologists!" This means consulting with a total of four doctors instead of two.

Regarding prevention: We know little about what causes cancer. However both Doctors said a good common sense diet and exercise can be beneficial. They were not particularly enthusiastic about holistic or alternative treatment. They feel there has not been any proof of success with any of these.

There has been disagreement among doctors on whether a man should be put on the CHT for a few months prior to surgery or radiation (called neoadjuvant therapy). The purpose of doing this is to reduce the size of the tumor in the prostate and the prostate gland itself, thus making the surgery or radiation easier to perform and even possibly increase the chances of success of both procedures. It may also help prevent the cancer from reaching the margins of the prostate capsule (this term is called positive margins) and possibly escaping into the bloodstream, thus making the surgery or the radiation useless.

The main disagreement seems to be among urologists. Some say "There is something bad that needs to be removed, why not do it right away and not waste any time?"

The opinions of Doctors Burke and Papadopoulos are interesting and seem to make sense. They say neither yes or no to the preliminary CHT (neoadjuvant) concept. "It depends on the individual," they said. If the doctor feels the prostate is not enlarged too much, he may proceed with treatment not using the prior CHT. If the prostate is enlarged to a certain point, then they feel it is best to administer the CHT for 3 months before surgery or radiation. This goes along with something we have known, that each individual case is different.

We have mentioned that the radiation equipment keeps getting better. It is fortunate that there are skilled experts such as these two doctors who are capable of effectively operating this equipment.

DR. ABRAHAM MITTELMAN: (Oncologist)
Associate Professor, New York Medical College, Valhalla N.Y.
"I am conducting experimental studies with a Chinese Herb, which I found out about from a patient who had a very high PSA, 1020, and after he started this herbal supplementation his PSA dropped dramatically to less then 1.

I asked for more information from the company who makes and distributes this product. They sent me information and I reviewed their patients with prostate cancer who were taking PC Spes. I reviewed their records and found out that when they started to take these herbs as a dietary supplementation their PSA levels dropped, so I got interested in this and I requested from the company to send me samples of PC Spes.

The company sent me samples and we had our cancer lab at the Medical College test it against prostate cancer cell lines that we have in the laboratory to see whether the herbs are effective in tissue culture. We found that PC Spes was killing prostate cancer cells in tissue culture.

So we got very interested and actually searched for the mechanism by which the herbs were working. It was effecting the cells dying process. In other words, it caused the cells to die by initiating a programmed cell death. We also tested it against a number of other cell lines. We looked to see if it was effective in breast cancer as well. We also looked for effectiveness in Neuroblastoma another tumor system. It was also effective in some of the breast cancer lines but not all of them. It was not effective against a skin cancer called Melanoma and did not appear to be very effective against some other cancers.

136

Interestingly enough, we found that if we treated the cancer cells with the herbs followed by chemotherapy, the results were much better then chemotherapy alone.

It is only used as a dietary supplementation and you can not tell your men in the Man to Man group that this is a cure or treatment for prostate cancer, because it is not.

So far I have monitored about ten patients. One of my patients had a PSA of 1200. He started to use the herbs as a dietary supplement and his PSA has dropped to 100. I have enough good data on five patients.

I have also spoken to the NIH (National Institute of Health). They have an office of alternative medicine and they expressed interest and asked me for some data which we plan to send them including all the laboratory findings we have so far. As soon as we have more patient information, we will send that too.

Men who have PCa, and have failed the CHT (combined hormonal therapy) and have failed other treatments, and there is nothing left for them, then I would like to see them. I would like to put these patients on this herbal dietary supplement. But they should first be given the opportunity to be treated with standard CHT and other drugs, and if they fail then we will try the herbs.

There are a total of eight herbs involved. I can tell you the names but I don't know what they mean. The portions that they are placed in is very important. They are in a capsule form and you must take three capsules three times a day as per company recommendation.

If this research proves positive it should be very promising in our battle against prostate cancer and other forms of cancer."

We would like to add a few comments to the above article concerning PC Spes by Dr. Mittelman: (Pc-Is the term for prostate cancer and Spes is a Chinese word for hope).

The research so far has been very limited. Most, if not all the subjects in his group, had used up all their medical options. There is certainly room for optimism when a man's PSA goes from over 1000 to 0. However, Dr. Mittelman and the company do not claim this is a cure for PCa or any other type of cancer. In fact the doctor does not state that PC Spes alone is a cure or a treatment for PCa.

On the other hand, the company must be very modest with their claims. Even though this is not sold in drug stores where the Food and Drug Administration must approve, they are sill under certain restrictions. For example the promotional booklet they put out only claims that PC Spes is a healthy herbal food supplement. The word "cancer" does not appear at all because of FDA restrictions. It is quite possible that due to restrictions, they are actually understating their product.

BOTANICLAB, producer of PC Spes makes no mention in their booklet or on the container of the capsule of any possible aftereffects. However, after speaking with the President of the company, we can confirm that there is at least one side effect, "disorders of the digestive tract." This should at least be on the label of the container. (If you have a reaction after taking any herb, call up the manufacturer). Some other aftereffects are tender breasts and occasional patients with blood clots (phlebitis).

We do not recommend or put down any product. Dennis O'Hara personally knows one of the men mentioned who had a 1020, PSA and takes the PC Spes. We both know of many other men who are taking this dietary supplement.

Sometimes certain things seem too good to be true, but on the other hand we must be open minded about any product that could be helpful be it medication or alternative.

DR. BERNARD SALEVITZ: (Urologist)
Dr. Bernard Salevitz is with a large urology group here in Dutchess County N.Y. He has had more experience with prostate cancer patients than most other doctors in this area.

Besides performing Radical Prostatectomy many times, he has prescribed just about every possible treatment. He has kept up with the latest trends regarding PCa and attends many seminars on this subject. He is now also doing Brachytherapy at our local hospital. Dr. Salevitz is the medical advisor for our Man to Man support group. We also appreciate the good doctor encouraging his patients to attend our Man to Man support group meetings where they have benefited tremendously.

Here is what Dr. Salevitz had to say in a very frank interview with our Dennis O'Hara, who was successfully operated on over 5 years ago by Dr. Salevitz.

"A lot of research has been done, but there is still a long road ahead. In spite of pre-op clinical staging for RP, including Bone scan, chest X-ray, Mri, and CAT scan, we have found approximately 35% of stage B have capsular penetration of cancer cells. This is because we still do not have a 100% way to detect cancer cells." He feels the recently heralded ProstaScint test that so many of us were optimistic about is not the big success it was originally believed to be. CAT scan and Bone scan are not as effective as many think.

Once a case becomes advanced, Dr. Salevitz points out there is no cut and dry course of treatment. It is all trial and error. The doctor must use his judgement based on a patient's age and history on which treatment to try. What helps one patient may not help another in which case something else is tried and hopefully you do not run out of options.

President Clinton recently took action to expedite time needed for FDA approval of certain drugs including cancer related drugs. Many promising drugs carry the notation that another few years is needed. Not all of us can wait that long. Dr. Salevitz along with the rest of us hopes that more effective means can be found for testing PCa patients so that proper methods of treatments can be more easily determined. Also that some effective treatment is developed soon that can at least keep advanced PCa under control.

Dr. Salevitz has spoken at our support group meetings and we have found him to be very knowledgeable and he has a wealth of information to share. We look forward to having him speak again in the near future. He has also given of his time and knowledge to the community by giving lectures on PCa at various health functions, and does a great service by performing screenings for PCa held at various hospitals in our community.

NAMES OF PHYSICIANS FAMILIAR WITH PC Spes

1. Dr. Josef Mendecki
    Atkin Center
    1052 E.55 St.
    New York, NY 10022
    Tel 212-758-2110
    Fax 212-755-2859

2. Dr. Abraham Mittelman
    Dept of Oncology Medicine
    New York Medical College
    Valhalla, NY 10595
    Tel 914-285-7514
    Fax 914-993-4420

3. Dr. Roy Berger
    Long Island, NY
    Tel 516-751-3000
    Fax 516-751-3553

4. Dr. Steven Strum
    Healing Oncology
    Culver City, CA
    Tel 310-558-4562
    Fax 310-558-1604

5. Dr. Israel Barkin
    San Diego, CA
    Tel 619-287-8866
    Fax 619-287-8890

6. One herbalist and nutritionalist, who treats cancer patients.
    Donald Yance Jr.
    Norwalk, Conn.
    Tel 203-849-8522
    Fax 203-849-1289

LATE DEVELOPMENTS

In September 1996, Time Magazine came out with a special fall edition dedicated to latest developments in the health field. Here is a summary from the section on cancer:

Virtually all anti cancer drugs interfere with cell division in some way. The problem with these drugs is they also kill off normal tissue. An example is the chemo cyclophosphamide which damages DNA molecules through triggering a suicide sequence. It causes the same suicidal result by deactivating a molecular machine that just before cell division separates the DNA in each chromosome into 2 separate strands.

I (Jules) can personally relate to the above. I was on Cyclophosphamide during January of 1996. It did not help and my PSA became very elevated. In the summer of 1996 I was put on Taxol which caused my PSA to drop.

NEW STRATEGY re. CANCER: Emphasis has been to eliminate cancer. This is especially true with prostate cancer where every book starts off with the need for early detection. Many now believe the time has come to concentrate more on containment, just what is needed for those of us who have PCa beyond Stages A & B. Recent development in this regard is a so called antiangiogenesis which makes colon, breast and prostate cancer shrink in mice. (LUCKY MICE)

What all this means is that in cancer cases where there is no so called cure in the foreseeable future every effort will be made to halt tumor growth and thus contain the cancer or to at least slow down tumor growth as much as possible.

Sloan-Kettering comes out with a bulletin which is sent to their patients and donors. I (Jules) am both. Some of the material is difficult for a laymen to understand.

This diagram is a good example. In plain language there are now (FEB, 1998) a number of promising vaccines to fight cancer. They are not taken as a pill, capsule or intravenously-but rather as an injection.

Anticancer vaccines stimulate antibodies and immune cells to attack tumor cells.

The anti-epidemal growth factor (EGF) receptor antibody blocks the blinding of EGF, which tumor cells need to continue dividing.

Antibodies such as the R24 monoclonal antibody mark tumor cells for destruction by the immune system.

Interleukin-2 and other immune boosters activate and stimulate the growth of immune cells, which attack tumor cells.

The main objective is to wipe out cancer cells while not hurting the "good guys." The big problem with chemo and sometimes radiation is that good cells are also destroyed.

So far the results of the vaccine tests are encouraging and this is not limited to just prostate cancer.

Dr. Phillip Livingston: At Memorial Sloan-Kettering has been working on vaccines for breast and prostate cancer for 3 years. As shown on diagram, the idea is to get the immune system to go after the "bad guys."

As of June 1997, the policy of Sloan-Kettering is to use this vaccine only for PCa patients who have had a recurrence after radical prostatectomy. Some other hospitals are using this vaccine for other advanced cases. Dr. Livingston is sure this vaccine will be shown to be completely effective within 2 years. UPDATE: Dec, 1997, Memorial Sloan Kettering is now using this vaccine on a wide variety of both prostate cancer and breast cancer patients.

Here is an Associated Press report dated October 21, 1996. No doubt there will be many more important developments after this book goes to press.

Journal of Science mentions a study where researchers report that a genetically engineered version of adenovirus-one of a number of viruses that cause the common cold-is able to attack and destroy human cancer cells that lack a gene called P53. Experiments on humans are already taking place. About half of all human cancers have a defective or missing P53 gene. 60% of human tumors grown in laboratory mice melted away with this treatment. Researchers at Johns Hopkins University are optimistic. Early experiments should conclude next spring.

From Associated Press dated October 23rd 1996: "Hormone may stop Cancers." A hormone is derived from urine of a pregnant woman. Direct injections into tumor often make the tumor disappear. This hormone apparently causes cancer cells to commit suicide.

This is thought to be effective against Kaposis Sarcoma- a form of cancer found mostly in AIDS patients. Studies are going on to see if this hormone can treat breast and prostate cancer.

Memorial Sloan Kettering hospital feels more study is needed before this treatment is used routinely for any type of cancer.

PROSTASCINT: A major advance in prostate cancer detection. ProstaScint is a product of a company named Cytogen. It is an innovative diagnostic imaging agent that is capable of accurately detecting prostate cancer. Much more than that, the extent and location of the PCa is determined. This represents a major advance. Millions of cases have been diagnosed before this, but there was often under staging or over staging the result being unnecessary surgery or radiation. Close to half the surgery did not succeed. With ProstaScint the patient can be much more accurately evaluated. ProstaScint can indicate when surgery or sometimes radiation is not appropriate.

We already have PSA's and biopsies to determine if a man has PCa. ProstaScint does much more. In addition to diagnosing, it is a big help in indicating appropriate treatment. We hope all doctors will be well informed regarding this special product. (FDA Approved October 1996).

ANOTHER LATE DEVELOPMENT: University of Texas scientists are destroying cancerous tumors in mice by engineering blood clots that starve the tumors to death. This could be tested in people within 2 years.

Results of tests on mice: Tumors disappeared in 38% of the mice and shrunk by more than half in another 24%. The basic idea is to clog vessels inside a tumor thus cutting off blood and oxygen needed by the tumor. The tumor would then die. The problem is they must be sure this would not cause any blood clots. The researchers are hoping to come up with a single drug to treat all tumors. Up until now different drugs are required for each type of tumor.

This therapy is not a cure-all. There is little risk of any serious side effects. There is a lot of optimism regarding this product. We can only hope that it will prove helpful and in the not too distant future.

Triprorelin: Is an LHRH agonist (see glossary). LHRH is a substance produced by the hypothalamus that regulates the production of sex hormones in both males and females. LHRH agonist currently marketed have been found to offer significant clinical benefit in and are widely used to treat conditions requiring the suppression of testosterone in males, such as prostatic cancer, or of estrogen in females, such as endometriosis.

VEPESID: (etoposide) Also commonly known as VP-16 is used in the treatment of "certain neoplastic diseases." "Neoplastic" in layman's language means a new tumor. The manufacturer, mentions specifically only two types of cancer: Small Cell Lung and Testicular.

However, a number of drugs accepted by FDA for other types of cancer are sometimes used to treat prostate cancer. A few of these are VePesid, Cyclophosphomate and Taxol. I (Jules) was put on the latter two. Cylcophosphomate did not help. Taxol did.

VePesid is a chemo drug. It can be administered either intravenously or orally by taking a 50 mg capsule. The one prostate cancer case I am aware of is D2 stage and he has hot spots on his backbone. He is taking this in the oral form. Each cancer cell can normally divide and form 2 new cells. The medical term for this is "mitosis." VePesid is designed to halt this process.

Each prostate cancer case is different. The doctor must use his discretion in determining treatment. One man may benefit, another may not. The only way you know for sure is to try the product.

Patients must be watched closely for any aftereffects when on VePesid. The main one is nausea. Only a small percentage have this problem and the treatment can then be cut back or terminated.

COLD VIRUS MAY STOP CANCER CELLS: Here is a bulletin from Associated Press dated March 25, 1997, Redston, Virginia. Twenty seven patients have received mutant cold viruses to infect their tumor cells and destroy them. The idea is to turn adenovirus, a usually mild mannered microbe that causes colds and intestinal upsets, into a kind of hunter that selectively attacks cancer cells that are fueled by a bad gene.

Over the past year, it has been tested mostly in people with terminally ill cancer in head and neck areas. A phase two study is intended to determine whether this treatment actually works. Cancers are triggered by a series of genetic mutations that make cells divide over and over. Often the last mutation to occur is one in the p53 tumor suppressor gene.

The researchers have created a form of the adenovirus that is missing the ability to disarm p53. So if it infects a healthy cell that is making normal amounts of p53 protein, it does nothing. But if it invades a cell that lacks p53, it will kill the cell and release more virus that in turn attacks neighboring cancer cells.

The technique appears to work well when the virus is injected into lab animals that have tumors. If all goes well with the head and neck experiments, it is hoped to try the treatments on bladder and liver cancer.

Later on hopefully it will be tried on other types of cancer such as prostate. It may become possible to give people yearly injections of the virus to cleanse the body of cells with bad p53 genes.

HYDRAZINE SULFATE: A Doctor, Joseph Gold has been working on Hydrazine Sulfate for about 20 years. He works practically alone and with very little financial assistance. This product also know as Seyhdrin, and "rocket fuel" is highly controversial. The "establishment" is not excited about it. Some claim the "establishment" would suffer financial loss if this was used instead of certain conventional chemotherapies.

There is no claim of a miracle cure. The claim is that this treatment could result in "positive symptomatic effects." We are talking about advanced cancer patients. There was an extensive test done on 740 patients between the ages of 16 and 72. By "positive improvement" they mean such things as general condition, decrease in fever, easier breathing, better appetite, less pain etc. The study claims those type of improvements in 54% of terminal cancer patients; 53% of Hodgkins patients; 44% of Breast cancer patients; 57% of Larynx patients. 71% of Neuroblastoma; (brain tumor) patients and 90% of those who had Desmosarcoma.

These were all patients who have advanced recurrent metastatic solid tumors and all other methods have been exhausted. Patients with 24 types of cancer (prostate cancer was not included) were tested and they claim 60% of these people showed some kind of progress.

It should be mentioned that this treatment is administered in tablet form and the tablet is very ***INEXPENSIVE***.

Is there a future for Seyhdrin (Hydrazine Sulfate-Rocket Fuel) ? We do not know at this time. Has the use of this product been hampered by the so called "establishment." It's possible, but this is not for us to determine.

TRIPLE ANDROGEN BLOCKADE: A doctor who has extensive experience and who is affiliated with PAACT (Patients Advocates for Advanced Prostate Cancer inc.) is optimistic about "Triple Hormone Blockade."

Normal CHT uses Zoladex or Lupron plus Eulexin or Casodex. The triple hormone blockade uses Eulexin not Casodex and Lupron or Zoladex but <u>adds</u> 5mg of Proscar (or finasteride) each day. The doctor believes this is a more aggressive treatment than the CHT and that aggressive treatment should be done "up front." He believes you must kill the greatest possible number of cancer cells on the first try.

This doctor claims his experience with using the triple treatment on an intermittent basis has resulted in improvement in quality of life and it may prolong life. He usually treats for a total of 13 months. On the negative side, this treatment could cause osteoporosis.

He mentions a new medication called Aredia (or pamidronate). This is to help patients who have had metastasis. It seems to be able to lower PSA and relieve pain, but it's not yet known whether this can prolong life. It is not a form of chemotherapy.

The doctor is bothered when someone calls him to say their doctor has informed them that nothing can be done for hormone refractory PCa. He says this is just NOT true!

SARASOTA MEMORIAL HOSPITAL: The Urology Treatment Center at this Hospital, located in Florida has recently announced a new compound known as PPI-149. This is a part of a new class of compounds known as LHRH antagonists. This is a new concept. The present two step Combination Hormone Treatment would be replaced by a single injection administered every three months. There would be a rapid reduction of serum testosterone and side effects are at a minimum.

We must emphasize that the above is experimental at this stage. Testing to obtain FDA approval is just beginning. There is no way of knowing when the FDA will act or if they will approve this particular procedure.

MEMORIAL SLOAN KETTERING; Dr. Howard Scher and Dr. Steven Larson have begun some research on a new scanning procedure called Positron Emission Tomography (PET Scan). It is being used for cases of advanced PCa. CAT scans and Bone scans can be helpful, but sometimes it is still difficult to find the cancer. PET scan may be better in finding the sight of metastases. Also it could help determine the types of energy (such as sugar) that the PCa is using to grow. As a result, treatment for patients can hopefully be improved. PET scan is a type of X-ray that uses two Radio tracer drugs to find out how active a tumor is and where it is located. PET Scan has been used in Breast & Brain Tumors.

The first drug Methionine, is injected into the body. A PET scan is done to see where the drug has moved in the body. The second drug, FDG or 18F deoxy-glucose is injected into the body. A second scan follows. The areas of possible cancer seen on PET scan are then compared to previous CAT and Bone scans already done.

The whole idea of PET scan is to learn more about any tumor and find out its exact location. Obviously treatment can then be more effective.

This is a fairly new procedure. It is not yet not in general use. It is being used experimentally at MSK Hospital on a limited number of volunteers. The results so far have been encouraging.

MEMORIAL SLOAN KETTERING: MSK recently has begun to evaluate a vaccine treatment for men who have refracted or failed treatment for their prostate cancer. The vaccine is based on an antigen called Globo H-KLH a carbohydrate molecule found in especially high numbers on the surface of many cancer cells.

The Globo H-KLH vaccine when given with an immune system stimulant, spurs the production of antibodies that attack tumor cells. In the new study, MSK researchers are testing 20 PCa patients who have already received surgery or radiation therapy, for their primary tumors.

Part 3

AFRICAN AMERICAN MEN

The reasons are not yet clear, but unfortunately the highest rate of prostate cancer in America is among African Americans. Their chances of getting this disease are 66% higher than for Caucasians.

Overall, African Americans have poorer survival rates for prostate cancer.

This is because about 32% of PCa in African Americans is diagnosed when already in advanced stages, compared to 19% for white men. Over 24% of African Americans diagnosed with PCa die of it. This is twice the rate of death compared to white American men. An important reason for this is the lack of awareness in the African American community of the importance of early detection.

Although reasons for PCa are unknown, some possibilities are being considered. Researchers are looking into genes, but have come up with nothing yet. There seems to be a tendency for this disease to appear more in some families. In that situation it is recommended that a man have a PSA done at age 40. Diet is also being considered. A high fat diet could be a factor. This is not certain.

On our local level here in Dutchess County New York, my co-author Dennis O'Hara has done his best to get more African Americans involved in our Man to Man support group. He has spoken to leaders of several African American churches, organizations and leading individuals in this area. He has also contacted top African American leaders on the national level to alert them to the danger PCa presents to the African American community and he suggests to these individuals that they spread the word.

Regardless of percentages, the key word here is INFORMATION. A lot more is needed for all men. This is the purpose of Man to Man and it is also the purpose of this book. With more information available, more lives can be saved. More men can make decisions regarding their treatment, not out of ignorance, but by making use of the knowledge that is available.

The leading cancer site for African American men during 1988-1992 was the prostate. All the reasons for this are net yet known. It has recently been suggested that African American men may at times require different types of treatment than White males. Much more research needs to be done on this.

Here are excerpts from a speech by Dr. Brian Stone, an African American Urologist, practicing in New York City. The speech was given at a prostate cancer leadership summit, September of 1996.

Four hundred cases of PCa were treated at Harlem Hospital between 1988 and 1993. 57% of these men already had a spread of cancer at time of diagnosis. 60% of those men had been under the care of a primary care physician who had failed to make the diagnosis. (One of the first things we emphasize at Man to Man is that PSA should be part of every Male's physical after age 50).

Dr. Stone said that "An African American male has a three times higher risk of dying from prostate cancer than a white male." This means he has an 85% greater chance of being diagnosed than whites.

Doctor Isaac Powell checked Veterans Administration system in Detroit. He found that with equal treatment, African Americans still had a higher mortality rate. He feels many African American men do not have early testing because there is extreme distrust of the medical establishment. Also there is a fear of the digital rectal-exam.

Everyone regardless of color has a fear of being diagnosed. He suggests ways of alerting the African American community such as cooperation by ministers. Also men who have been diagnosed should spread the word. Of course this is exactly what Man to Man is all about!

A study was done of men with prostate cancer who were less than 50 years of age when diagnosed. There was a higher risk of dying for African Americans in this category. A point: In the case of married men, it's important to get cooperation of the wives. They can help convince the men to have early screening. Perhaps more of an effort should be made to reach out to them.

Politicians and insurance companies are constantly trying to cut down the costs of health care. It's important for each person (whether it is prostate cancer or another illness) to be treated regardless of his or her insurance coverage or personal finances.

Some insurance companies are thinking of eliminating such things as PSA test from their coverage. This is something Man to Man is watching.

Just recently Dennis and I (Jules) had an audience with a New York State Senator. We wanted to know what funds if any the state is allocating for PCa research. Man to Man is also constantly trying to have legislation enacted in each state that would require the doctor to fully inform each PCa patient. This means letting a person know all the options available for treatment, chances of success, and any possible aftereffects. Also, to keep the patient informed of all test results.

We are not giving up on our African American brothers. We plan to appear at more churches and to contact more local people. Hopefully, if the word gets out in Dutchess County New York, it will spread from here to other places.

From computer health bulletin board-April 1997: A research team at Johns Hopkins Hospital, has come up with preliminary evidence that a certain gene dubbed (Hereditary Prostate Cancer Gene #1 taken from the first chromosome from our bodies of which there are 23) HPC-1 appears to cause about one third of all inherited PCa. Most PCa happens sporadically and there is no family history. HPC-1 is a damaged gene that passes from one generation to another and plays a key role in triggering PCa. In about 30% of cases where PCa occurs in a family, HPC-1 is a factor. This factor appears much more in black than in white families.

It's still too early to say for sure, but this is certainly strong evidence that at least one reason has been uncovered for the predominance of PCa among African Americans. There is also a tendency for those (black or white) who have the bad gene to develop PCa at an earlier age, 64 as opposed to the average age of 72 for men who do not have the inherited disease. More research is being done.

From a Booklet entitled "Cancer Facts & Figures for African Americans" put out by the American Cancer Society:

African Americans have a higher incidence of Cancer than the white population. Cancer is second only to heart disease as a leading cause of death among African American Men. In 1996 33,830 African American men died of Cancer. 10,700 (32%) died from lung cancer, the number 1 cancer killer. 6,400 died from Prostate Cancer or 19%.

The 5 year survival rate for PCa among the white population is 88%. 5 year survival rate for African Americans is 71%-considerably lower.

I (Dennis) recently attended a landmark Leadership Conference on Prostate Cancer in African Americans, Houston Texas (Nov.19-23, 1997) aimed specifically at making the Black community more aware of PCa. Many leaders from across America attended.

The ACS, NCI, CDC, put this together in conjunction with the Intercultural Cancer Council, the 100 Black Men of America, the National Black Leadership Initiative on Cancer, and the National Prostate Cancer Coalition.

Some very important African American men spoke in reference to this problem in the Black communities across America. Among them was Dr. Issac J. Powell, a urological oncologist and associate professor at Wayne State University and himself a recent survivor of PCa. Dr. Otis Brawley from the National Cancer Institute. Lovell A. Jones, Ph.D. from The University Of Texas, MD Anderson Cancer Institute. Dr. Brian Stone urologist from Columbia Presbyterian Medical Center, NY City and many, many more.

These dedicated professional and lay people all came together to try and set up a National Blueprint For Action so to speak to reach the Black Communities and to inform them about Prostate Cancer.

I was honored to be invited and be among these great men and women who were Scientists, Doctors, lay people both Black and White. I would like to thank the ACS and all the people at this his-torical gathering for allowing me to attend and also to be treated as an equal and for listening to me as a survivor and an advocate for PCa both in the White community and the Black community.

This was not a fun and games holiday paid for by the ACS, as a matter of fact it was a very intense 3 day series of serious PCa related meetings on detection and education of PCa in America, with the emphasis on African Americans.

There were many work shops addressing this problem and I in particular came away with a lot of innovative ideas on how to reach our Black community here in Dutchess County NY.

One evening a play called "A Matter of Manhood" by Thomas Meloncon, was presented to us. I enjoyed it tremendously and it was very well put together. An all Black cast gave a message to Black Americans on how important it is to get screened and to followup with your doctor about the results. There were not too many dry eyes that night mine included. Here in NY I am in the process of trying to get that play and to followup with a PCa screening for the Black men in our community.

The Black Ministers in our area have been contacted and with the help of the ACS and other groups, we hope to make this happen.

Position Statement from the Urology Section of The National Medical Association

Since the mortality rate from prostate cancer between the ages of 45 and 70 is 2 to 3 times greater among African Americans compared to Caucasians, we propose that African Americans within those age ranges who have a life expectancy of at least 10 years should have DRE and PSA testing. Testing should be accompanied by education about the benefits and risks of treatment.

American Cancer Society Draft Guide lines and Narrative For The Detection Of Early Prostate Cancer

Guideline Statement.
Both Prostate-Specific Antigen (PSA) and Digital Rectal Examination (DRE) should be offered annually, beginning at age 50 years, to men who have at least a 10-year life expectancy, and to younger men who are at high risk.

Late Developments

CPDR (Center for Prostate Disease Research) has done a study. It shows that African American men with PCa exhibited higher PSA levels at every stage, grade, age and tumor value.

The CPDR therefore developed age specific reference ranges for maximal cancer detection in African American men. These new ranges help to maximize cancer detection in African American men. Thus African American men stand a better chance of being diagnosed at earlier more treatable stages.

Walter Reed/Center for Prostate Research (WR/CPDR Age-Adjusted PSA Ranges for Maximum Cancer Detection

Age	African American	Caucasian	Traditional PSA "Normal" for All Men	Traditional Age-Adjusted References Ranges Based on Caucasian Men (Mayo Clinic)*
40-49	0-2.0	0-2.5	0-4.0	0-2.5
50-59	0-4.0	0-3.5	0-4.0	0-3.5
60-69	0-4.5	0-3.5	0-4.0	0-4.5
70-79	0-5.5	0-3.5	0-4.0	0-6.5

*JAMA 1993; 270:860   Fall 1997 Family Urology 9

AMERICAN CANCER SOCIETY

In 1913 an organization called The American Society for the Control of Cancer was founded in New York City.

Today we know this organization as the American Cancer Society (ACS).

Doctors felt there was no way to educate Women about Cervical Cancer, which at that time was considered incurable.

During the 20's & 30's many changes and expansions took place, like the recruitment of medical and laymen volunteers, and most of the programs the American Cancer Society has today as we know them, emerged during this period.

In the 1950's 60's and 70's early detection, anti tobacco, and the advocacy for cancer control originated. Also in 1971 President Nixon signed The National Cancer Act, along with the ACS leadership and it is still today the strength behind all of the ACS cancer control efforts.

During the 1980's the Breast Cancer Support Group concept originated and it was at this point that the men's support group system can be traced to. It was started to help their spouses deal with breast cancer.

In the 1980's the ACS realized that prostate cancer was in need of more research, treatments and early detection; in addition, a male support group was started.

In the early 1990's the Man to Man support groups were founded by Jim Mullens of Sarasota Florida. The ACS adopted the Man to Man concept around the same time and Man to Man became affiliated with the ACS. Our mission is to try and get men to come out socially to share with each other their experiences and emotions concerning prostate cancer, and to pass along any information we have.

The breast cancer support groups were very successful, and as the founder (Dennis) and facilitator of a very active local Man to Man group, I can tell you Man to Man will also be very successful in getting the word out about prostate cancer. All men will become advocates for this cancer killer of men. In 1998 over 40,000 will die of it.

At a National Assembly meeting on November 3, 1996 the ACS identified prostate cancer as a leading priority for their units.

The ACS is staffed by many dedicated paid and unpaid volunteers, many of them unsung heroes. At our local ACS here in Dutchess County N.Y. people, like Cathy Close, have given me and our support group so much of their time and patience to help form our Man to Man group.

I know at times I have driven her to the point of complete exhaustion and frustration with my off-the-wall requests for our support group, and constant phone calls regarding prostate cancer and Man to Man. But she and all of the other people at the ACS are to be commended. Without them most support groups would not be. They provide the funds and most of what we need to continue. On behalf of survivors everywhere, I take my hat off to you all, and say to the American Cancer Society, "Thank you."

Here is a list of some important phone numbers you must have in your library on Prostate Cancer.

American Cancer Society (MAN TO MAN) Support & Information
800-ACS-2345 (local offices in white pages of phone book)

American Foundation for Urological Disease
800-828-7866 / 410-468-1800

American Institute for Cancer Research
800-843-8114 (nutrition hot line)

Cancer Care
800-813-HOPE

Cancer Research Institute
800-99-CANCER

Cap Cure (Association for The Cure of Cancer Of The Prostate)
800-757-2873

Mathews Foundation for Prostate Cancer Research
800-234-6284

Memorial Sloan-Kettering Diagnostic Center (N.Y.City)
212-639-4703

National Cancer Institute (NCI)
800-4-CANCER

National Coalition for Cancer Survivorship
301-650-8868

Prostate Cancer Survivor Network (US-TOO)
800-808-7866

Patients Advocates for Advanced Cancer Treatment (PAACT)
616-453-1477

Prostate Cancer Genetic Research Study (PROGRESS)
800-777-3035

R.A. Bloch Cancer Foundation, Inc.
816-932-8453

The above listings represent only a small number of organizations that are available to help you with prostate cancer
information, and cancer information in general. Most of them
have fax numbers, are on line and have E mail addresses.

There are many excellent local organizations, too numerous
to list. To locate them, call your local cancer treatment center
or your local American Cancer Society.

A word about the ACS, the sponsor of our Man To Man support group. It is nation wide. Its goal is to find a cure for cancer, mainly thru research.

Here are some very vital statistics listed by the ACS regarding cancer in general: Four out of every ten cancer patients
will live at least five years after being diagnosed. In the early
1900's very few had any hope of long term survival. Ten million Americans who have a cancer history are still alive. Seven
million of these were diagnosed five or more years ago.

The above numbers show what a huge national challenge
cancer is. It also shows there is "hope for the future" (a chapter in this book).

Regarding prostate cancer, the survival rate is better than
many other types of cancer. However, it is projected that
there will be 200,000 new cases in 1998. Obviously efforts
must be intensified until a cure is finally found.

At a PCa symposium held in Houston, Texas 11/19-23, 1997, a statement was made by top leaders from the ACS. "It is our goal at the ACS by the year 2015 to reduce the mortality rate from PCa by 50%."

Here are some interesting facts regarding cancer in general, prostate cancer and AIDS.

Funding For 1996

	# OF DEATHS	$ INVESTMENT
Aids	51,000	$ 1.62Billion
Breast Cancer	45,000	$ 550 Million
All Cancer Research by U.S. Govt.	550,000	$ 2.6 Billion
Prostate cancer by U.S. Govt.	41,000	$ 60-80 Million

We have pretty much avoided statistics, but these are numbers everyone should be aware of. During the past decade more than 12 million new cases of cancer were diagnosed. More than 1.5 million of these were prostate cancer. The U.S. spent $2 trillion on defense, including $2.6 billion for each new stealth bomber. $73 billion spent on space programs, and only $12 billion on cancer- 2% of this on prostate cancer research.

CONCLUSION: Government must invest much more for cancer research in general and for prostate cancer research in particular. Cancer research amounts to 1/10 of 1% of our federal budget!

FOUNDATION, INSTITUTIONS AND PRIVATE ASSOCIATIONS WORKING TO CURE PROSTATE CANCER

Cap Cure

Cap Cure is the association for the cure of cancer of the prostate. This group was founded by Michael Milken who is the President. The Milken family foundation has been generous, they are committed to donate 25 million dollars over a period of time.

From 1993 to 1995 Cap Cure has donated $19,563,000 to various hospitals and universities. This research is strictly for PCa and nothing else. Some of the larger donations were: Over $1,000,000 to each of the following institutions, Baylor College of Medicine, Harvard Medical School, Johns Hopkins University, Memorial Sloan Kettering, University of Texas, University of Washington.

Cap Cure claims that all money you donate will go directly to research. The reason for this is that any money needed for administrative expenses comes from funds donated by the Milken foundation.

It is difficult to describe the exact type of research each one of these institutions is doing because there are so many medical terms. However, we will mention what is happening at a few where PCa is being researched.

Baylor College of Medicine

Molecular Markers for PCa progression. Also gene therapy including the role of androgen receptor genes in restricting advanced PCa.

Dana Farber

Also working on androgen receptors.

Johns Hopkins

Working on a vaccine that targets Endothelin Axis in treatment of metastatic PCa.

Memorial Sloan Kettering

Half a dozen projects including development of polyvalent vaccine for PCa.

Washington University

The role of Corepressor NABZ in PCa.

HOSPITALS AND DOCTORS

Some people are interested in knowing which are the best doctors and hospitals. U.S. News & World Report does an annual analysis on hospitals. They are rated in various categories.

The first nine are in the same order as 1995. This latest issue covering their analysis is dated August 12, 1996. Taken into account are opinions of doctors, death rate statistics, technology-meaning quality of imaging equipment, radiation equipment, scanning devices, etc. and the quality of care. Here is how they are ranked.

1-Memorial Sloan Kettering Cancer Center- New York
2-University of Texas, M.D. Anderson Cancer Center-Houston
3-Dana-Farber Cancer Institute-Boston
4-Johns Hopkins Hospital-Baltimore MD.
5-Mayo Clinic-Rochester, Minn.
6-Stanford University Hospital-Stanford, California
7-University of Washington, Medical Center-Seattle
8-University of Chicago Hospitals
9-University of California, San Francisco Medical Center
10-Massachusetts General Hospital-Boston
11-Roswell Park Cancer Institute-Buffalo N.Y.
12-Indiana University Medical Center-Indianapolis

SPECIALIST IN PROSTATE CANCER

Regarding Doctors: There is a book called "The Best Doctors in America." This book costs about $85. The book is by Steven Naifeh and Gregory White Smith. Most of the data to compose these names came from interviewing the doctors themselves.

Of course we will confine our listing to doctors who specialize in prostate cancer. The book on best doctors came out with much shorter lists in each category than the hospital listings. There are many good doctors who are not listed, but if one is in the book, he has to be pretty good.

The following are doctor who specialize in Prostate Cancer:

Howard Scher: Memorial Sloan-Kettering Cancer Center. (He happens to be my doctor) (Jules)

George Wilding: He is assistant professor of human oncology and medicine at Wisconsin -Madison School of Medicine and University of Wisconsin Comprehensive Cancer Center.

Frederick Ahmann: He is associate professor of medicine at University of Arizona College of Medicine. Also he is chief of their hematology and oncology section.

Mario Eisenberg: Associate professor of medicine and oncology at the University of Maryland School of Medicine-University of Maryland Cancer Center.

L. Michael Glode: Professor of Medicine at Division of Medical Oncology, University of Colorado School of Medicine-University of Colorado Health Sciences Center.

David Johnson: Associate Professor of Medicine, Division of Medical Oncology, Vanderbilt University School of Medicine Vanderbilt University Medical Center.

Patrick Walsh: Not mentioned in this book on "top doctors," but probably one of the best known prostate cancer specialists in the country is Dr. Patrick Walsh who is at Johns Hopkins in Baltimore Maryland. He is a top surgeon who has probably performed more prostate surgery than almost anyone. A few men in our Man to Man support group were operated on by Dr. Walsh. One person had a recurrence. He is known for the fact that he originated the nerve sparing procedure whereby nerve endings are sometimes preserved, thus enabling continuation of a normal sex life. By now many other doctors are capable of doing this. He is no doubt one of the best at what he does.

As mentioned previously, most of this book is taken up with the challenge of those who are the more advanced cases of prostate cancer. These men, including myself, (Jules) are dependent on whatever is available right now and hope and pray that there will be new medications in the future that will prolong our lives even more.

REGARDING ADVANCED CASES

Some doctors write these off as hopeless and almost always want nothing to do with these men. These doctors are interested in one thing, performing as much surgery as possible. Surgery is appropriate in some cases. To us the real heroes are the doctors who keep trying to help the advanced cases. This is the real challenge of the future and we in the support groups applaud these physicians.

There are many medical books about PCa with all sorts of statistics. These numbers can be very depressing and since each case is different these numbers generally do not mean anything to the individual.

As an example the statistics show few stage "D2" survive 5 years. Yet doctors report many of these men survive 5 years or even 10 years. The statistics show average life expectancy of a person with Gleason score of 9 or 10 is 2 years. Yet many of these men including myself, (Jules) are here much longer. My doctor (Scher) has dealt with many cases like mine. When I asked him what my outlook is, based on statistics, he said there is no way of telling because each person is different and these statistics would be of no help to me.

There are some vital statistics we would like to see, such as how many of those 41,000 plus men who die each year with PCa were over 75 years old. Also, how many of them were diagnosed too late, and how many were in a small town and might have been helped if they had gone to a place like Memorial Sloan-Kettering. We have pretty much avoided statistics in this book. Instead we have emphasized the possibility of new treatments that may prolong life.

Here are numbers that present a positive picture: There are 2 million known PCa cases in the U.S.A. and over 41,000 deaths each year. This means about 1 man with PCa out of fifty will die during 1998. Of course it's sad about the 41,000, but at least a person's odds are good. This brings us back to the old saying that a man with PCa is likely to die from something else; "Die with PCa not from it."

Our support group, "Man to Man," has been in existence for over 4 years now and we never discuss statistics. We are very positive and talk only about possible cures. Anyone who has been told that a support group meeting is a depressing experience should attend a meeting and find out for himself. Better yet, we invite you to come to one of our meetings, and we can assure you it will be a very rewarding, life extending experience. Also don't forget to bring your wife or significant other so they can experience our sister group Side by Side.

Review of past year by Jules Schwartz
Personal and Significant developments.

Personal: It is now February 1998, over a year since we began this book. I am on Zoladex. Also taking Maitake mushroom and Modified citrus pectin. My PSA is 130. I have some hot spots on my spine and a small tumor on my right hip. I have received Strontium 89 and will presently get 12 treatments of external beam radiation.

I will soon be joining the 88% of Caucasians who survive PCa for the first five years. Unfortunately the number of Afro-Americans who survive for five years is only 71%.

I am optimistic about my future health-wise and continue to feel good and live an active lifestyle.

One sunny day in Sept. Sandy and I were out for lunch at a local quaint inn. I am a slow eater so Sandy decided to browse at the local stores while I finished eating. After lunch I had to make a pit stop at the bathroom and while standing at the urinal and voiding, blood gushed out all over the place. What a shock! It scared the daylights out of me. Nothing like this has ever happened to me.

I mentioned it to Sandy and we both thought it was from the radiation treatment I had just about 2 hours before lunch. It did clear up a few days later. This had occurred on Wednesday.

The following Tuesday blood again appeared in my urine. That night I got up every 5 minutes and passed blood. The next morning one week after the initial bleeding, I could not urinate and went to the hospital. I saw Dr. Burke, who is a radiation oncologist and quoted in "Doctor's Opinions." He noticed a urologist passing by, Dr. Lieberman. He is the senior partner of a large urology group her in Poughkeepsie. Dr. Lieberman is the original doctor who diagnosed me with PCa. I was lucky that he was there, he immediately put me into the emergency room. The problem was two fold. My prostate gland was bleeding into the bladder, the blood was clotting - thus blocking off the flow of urine. He irrigated my bladder and used a suction tool to remove blood, all this done thru a catheter tube. I was then admitted to the hospital. The following day the important procedure was done, my bladder was again cleaned out and then using a laser, the prostate gland was cauterized-thus stopping the bleeding.

I am fine again and spent a week in the hospital. This is a good example of how you can be going along fine and something unexpectantly comes up. If you ever have blood appear in your urine, have this checked at once.

The condition referred to above is called "Hematuria." This has happened to me four times within the last five months. There seems to be another procedure that can be done to hopefully correct this problem. It is called Transurethral Resection of The Prostate (TURP) or as we call it in laymens term a "Roto Rootor." This procedure will scrape away the part of the prostate that is bleeding and should correct the problem I am probably going to have this. TURP is also done in cases of an enlarged prostate (BPH). All of the above terms are in the glossary.

APRIL 1998: A Pet Scan was done at MSK and it showed some new hot spots in my groin area. Dr. Scher started me on an experimental chemo treatment. Once a week for six weeks. After only 2 treatments I was admitted to the hospital for Hematuria again. In the hospital an intestinal perforation was found, which may have been caused by the chemo. It resulted in a serious infection. It lasted for 13 days. I am presently awake and alert and looking forward to going home.

Review of past year by Dennis O'Hara

Personal and Support Group/Man to Man.

Personal: My situation as of January 1998. I am feeling pretty good. The Lyme disease battle has finally turned in my favor, after 18 months of treatment with both weekly injections of Bicillan and heavy daily doses of oral antibiotics, I am almost back to being a member of the human race. I can truthfully say that the Lyme disease has given me more physical problems than the Prostate Cancer and maybe someday I will write a book on that subject!

I have passed a milestone like Jules, and have completed my fifth year as a survivor of PCa. March of 1998 will be the six year mark.

I have had PSA's every three months for the first three years then at year four it went to every four months and at five years every six months. Up until July 15, 1997, all my PSA's have been less 0.1. The latest PSA was less then 0.5. A slight elevation but a significant one. I have done some investigation and discovered that the hospital that I have been using has changed labs, and upon questioning the lab I discovered that they did not take the specimen down to "zero" so I must be retested again.

It seems that the hospital changes labs every 6 to 8 months because of economics. Some labs will do PSA much cheaper than others. Always keep up on your lab and find out who does the analyzing and what their values are, and make sure if you have had a RP, and your doctor prescribes a PSA for you, the RX should state that this is a PSA following a Radical Prostatectomy and the code number HO8-O should appear on the RX. This code tells the lab this is not an ordinary PSA but a PSA that should be analyzed to the lowest level "zero."

GOOD NEWS!!! The repeat PSA came back <0.1. Date of this PSA was 8/12/1997. It seems the lab did not read the RX and follow the instructions to analyze the blood sample to lowest value.

LOTS OF GOOD NEWS!!!

PSA 2/98 <0.1. Bone scan same date also no change since 1992. Hallelujah, Praise God.

SUPPORT GROUP/MAN to MAN:

Another milestone has been reached here also, we are now entering our fifth year. Our support group has been meeting since July of 1993. We have over 150 active members and at least that many inactive.

When I started the Poughkeepsie Man to Man support group there were only a handful of prostate cancer support groups across the nation, today there are over 300.

During the five year period, only 10 men have gone to the great support group in the sky, and out of that 10 only 4 to PCa. A pretty good track record.

I am not trying to mislead you about living and dying but just telling you how it is. It is a proven fact that when you are faced with a serious illness, people live longer and happier when they belong to a support group.

We continue to give moral support and important information in the form of a newsletter and many handouts concerning the latest breakthroughs in regards to PCa. The personal experiences of every member are a wealth of information that we all share. At every meeting there are at least 4 to 5 new men seeking help. No one goes away with the attitude that all is lost and he is going to die.

Every three months or so we have special speakers, the latest was Dr. Sophie Chen, she is one of the scientist who has developed PC Spes, a dietary supplement which seems to bring the PSA down and in some cases it actually shrinks the PCa tumors.

We have had many important speakers, some from drug companies, some from local hospitals, some of our local doctors. A lawyer once spoke on what the law was all about in regards to our medical reports and what the medical professionals are legally bound to tell us. We also have had a chiropractor, an alternative PHD, and a Lyme disease specialist and the list goes on and on.

Attitude is just as important as physical condition when you are fighting any disease, especially cancer. Our meetings are always positive and upbeat and I personally have never acted like a funeral director. The group has a big impact on the lives of men and their families. I know this to be a fact as many, many men and their families have come up to me and told me so. Some of our men have been to other PCa support across the country and they tell me our meetings are the best. These statements make it all worth while.

I like Jules, continue to be very optimistic about my health and will continue to be an advocate for PCa. On September 23, 1997 I attended a special Senate hearing in Washington DC. Bob Dole and many other well known men spoke on how our government needs to have more money allocated for PCa. research. There were about 30 men representing M2M support groups from all over the country present with me. The ACS and American Federation for Urologic Disease sponsored this lobbying effort in conjunction with National Prostate Cancer Awareness Week.

One of my other tasks that day was to contact my New York State leaders in Washington and to urge them to give us more money for research and detection and prevention of PCa. I now urge all of you who read this book to contact your state leaders and urge them to do the same.

There are so many studies and treatments going on, and so many dedicated people who are trying to find a cure for PCa that I feel we are only a few years away from a major breakthrough for PCa.

I also feel that the breakthrough will come from the holistic side, working with the medical community.

ACTION NEEDED

Tell President Clinton:

"Make Prostate Cancer a National Priority"

Write: OR CALL:

President Bill Clinton   White House Comments Line

The White House   (202) 456-1414

1600 Pennsylvania Avenue N.W.

WASHINGTON, DC 20500

Above is from the National Prostate Cancer Coalition newsletter. NPCC Web Site # is www.4npcc.org

SIDE BY SIDE

My wife Jackie continues to facilitate the Side by Side support group for the female counterparts of PCa survivors. Her group is getting stronger at every meeting and very well attended. The ladies seem to enjoy this concept and feel that they are not kept in the dark in reference to PCa. They also enjoy the speakers and look forward to the information that is passed around.

Jackie does a good job heading up this group and Man to Man really appreciates her efforts, thanks Jack!!!

OBSERVATION:

Jackie and the other women in Side by Side are the most important support system for their husbands. Both Jules and I have mentioned that we personally could not have done without this support system.

An interesting note in this regard is that there was a little publicized report in "The Journal of Urology," November 1996. They did a detailed study of 146,979 men who had prostate cancer. The study covers time period of 1973 to 1990. Result: Married patients had significantly longer median survival than those who were single, divorced, separated or widowed.

Doctors agree that mental health is important in dealing with any illness. Obviously if a man has a good marriage, his mate will be his number one support system. As mentioned, Side by Side is made up of such women.

YOU ARE IMPORTANT

There are many good prostate cancer doctors. Many of these are at prestigious places like Columbia Presbyterian, Memorial Sloan-Kettering and Johns Hopkins. When you read the various biographies in this book you will see that some men received appropriate treatment and are doing well.

The problem comes into play when a man goes beyond stage "B" prostate cancer to enter "advanced stages." There is no set treatment for everyone except the Combined Hormonal Therapy. However this eventually wears off. Many of these men have too little treatment, too much, or improper treatment.

The medical profession must clean up its act. If a doctor is treating PCa he should be well informed including latest developments and he should use sound judgement. He has a duty to fully inform his patient of all possible treatments and all possible consequences. Also he has an obligation to keep a patient fully informed on all test results.

Regarding the patient, remember you are responsible for your own body. Any final decisions are up to you. It's up to you to question the doctor. You are not only entitled to test results, but as Dennis O'Hara points out, you can ask for the results in writing. These test results are important in case you must get another opinion or should you choose another doctor. He or she can use them to determine any further treatment.

If you have any doubts about your doctor, see someone else. Don't worry about the doctors feelings. And no matter how good your doctor is, always get a second, or in some cases a third opinion. For the second or third opinion, you might want to go out of your area to a different medical community.

Our Man to Man support group is small compared to many others. Nevertheless the cases we have of misjudgment are probably repeated many times throughout this country.

Prostate Cancer Support Groups

Confronting dilemmas of prostate cancer is easier if you can share the road with other people who can say, "I understand, I've been there and have had the same fears and concerns." Support groups offer the opportunity to be with other prostate cancer survivors and their families.

Prostate cancer support groups normally involve peer support and education through presentations by medical professionals and lay persons. Each group will function according to the needs and resources of its particular area.

In 1991, there were only a handful of local groups across the country that were dedicated solely to prostate cancer support and education. As of this printing, the locations of almost 300 local support groups have been verified 286, to be exact.

If a specific group has not been included or if there are changes, please notify the Prostate Cancer Network of AFUD. at 410-468-1800. This list will be revised regularly due to the formation of new groups, changes in leadership and sometimes the dissolution of a particular group.

The above and the following list of support groups nationwide is used with the permission of the American Federation for Urologic Disease (AFUD).

ALABAMA

Birmingham
Prostate Cancer Support Group
University of Alabama at Birmingham
205-934-1464
205 975-8767

Dothan
US TOO Prostate Support Group S.E.
Alabama Medical Center
334-794-3216

Wiregrass US TOO Prostate Cancer
Support Group
205-794 4159

Florence
Florence Prostate Cancer
Support Group
205-776-9764

Mobile
US TOO Prostate Cancer
Support Group
205-343-9090

ALASKA

Anchorage
US TOO Prostate Cancer Group—
Alaska
907-276-2803

ARIZONA

Dewey
US TOO Prostate Cancer Support
Group— Northern AZ
520-445-4564

Flagstaff
Flagstaff Prostate Cancer
Support Group
520-779-5547

Fountain Hill
Prostate Cancer Support Groups—
Arizona
602-837-8728

Glendale
US TOO of Glendale Arrowhead Cancer
Center
602-274-4484

Lake Havasu City
US TOO Prostate Cancer
Support Group
520-855-6833

Nogales
Santa Cruz Prostate Cancer
Support Group
520-761 -3103

Scottsdale
US TOO Prostate Support Group
602-991 -0821

Sierra Vista
US TOO Prostate Cancer
Support Group
602-459-2392

Sun City West
US TOO Prostate Cancer Support
Group— Phoenix
602-546-0079

ARKANSAS

Fayetteville
Fayetteville Prostate Cancer
Support Group
501 -521 -8980

Springdale
Prostate Cancer Support Group
800-458-8954

US TOO Support Group of Northwest Arkansas North Arkansas Radiation Therapy Institute
501-751-2480

CALIFORNIA

Fresno
Prostate Cancer Support Group
Community Hospital of Central California
209-244-6133

Fullerton
Prostate Forum
714 526-3793

Huntington Beach
Prostate Cancer Support Group
Long Beach
714-969-2388

Livermore
Tri Valley Prostate Cancer Support 510-447-8965

Los Angeles
Discussion and Education Group—UCLA
310-825-5538

UCLA School of Medicine
310-825 5538

Loma Linda
Loma Linda Medical Center Prostate Cancer Support
800-782-2623

Monterey
Prostate Cancer Self-Help Group of Monterey
408-373-5915

Orange
Prostate Cancer Forum
714-633-9241

Palm Springs
Prostate Cancer Support Group—Palm Springs Desert Hospital Comprehensive Cancer Center
619-323-6831

Pasadena
Prostate Cancer Support Group
Foothills Wellness Center
818-796-1083

Pomona
Prostate Cancer Support Group
Pomona Valley Hospital
909-865-9517

Rancho Mirage
Eisenhower Memorial Hospital Prostate Support
310-376-3550

Riverside
Men and Prostate Cancer Riverside Medical Foundation
714-682-2753

San Diego
San Diego Prostate Cancer Support Group
619-286-3520
619-287-8866

San Francisco
US TOO Prostate Cancer Support and Education Group Dept of Veteran Affairs Medical Center
415-221 4810 x 2103

Prostate Concerns Support Group
415-387-0961

Santa Barbara
US TOO—Cancer Foundation
805-969-7166

Prostate Cancer Discussion Group
Cancer Foundation of Santa Barbara
805-682-7300

Santa Monica
Prostate Cancer Support of Santa
Monica Westside Wellness Community
310-314-2555

San Pablo
Brookside Hospital Prostate Support
510-235-1137

Sherman Oaks
Sherman Oaks Hospital and Health
Center
818-981-7111
818-589-4517

Thousand Oaks
US TOO Prostate Cancer Support
Group Thousand Oaks/Columbia/Los
Robles Hospital
805-379-5588

Willows
Man-to-Man Prostate Cancer
Support Group
916-934-3993

Woodland Hills
Woodland Hills Prostate Cancer
Support Group Kaiser Permanente
Medical Center
818-719-3785

COLORADO

Denver
Man-to-Man Prostate Cancer Support
Group American Cancer Society—CO
Division
303-759-2030

CONNECTICUT

Hartford
Hartford Hospital Prostate Cancer
Support Group
860-545-3790

St. Francis Hospital Prostate Support
860-714-4214

Meriden
Prostate Cancer Support Group
Veterans Memorial Medical Center
203-238-8401

New London
Man-to-Man Prostate Support Group
American Cancer Society
203-887-2547

Waterbury
Urology Specialists Prostate Support
Group
203-757-8361

DELAWARE

Milford
Southern Delaware Prostate Cancer
Support Group
302-422-7032
302-442-2010

Wilmington
Prostate Cancer Support Group
302-478-3530

FLORIDA

Clearwater
Clearwater Prostate Cancer Support
Group
813-443-4505

Coral Springs
Coral Springs Prostate Cancer Support
Group
954-755-3801

Delray Beach
Delray Medical Center Prostate Support
Group
561-495-3335

Ft. Lauderdale
I Will Manage Prostate Support North
Ridge Medical Center
954-776-6000 x 4879

Hollywood
Memorial Hospital Prostate Cancer
Support Group
954 985-3435

Kissimmee
Man-to-Man Prostate Cancer Support
Group
407-933-8525

Marathon
US TOO Florida Keys
305-743 6526

Margate
US TOO—Northwest Regional Hospital
954-979-2444

Miami
Man-to-Man Prostate Support Group—
Miami
305-547-2210

North Miami Beach
Aventura/North Dade Prostate Cancer
Support Group
305-654 4460

Palm Coast
Man-to-Man—Prostate Cancer Support
Group
904-445-1701

Pensacola
Man-to-Man Prostate Cancer Support
Group
904-438-4491

Pompano Beach
Prostate Support Group North Broward
Medical Center
954-786-6460

Rome
Prostate Cancer Education and Support
Group Redmond Regional Medical
Center
706-291 -0291

Saint Augustine
Florida Cancer Center Prostate Support
Group
904-824-5189

Saint Petersburg
St. Petersburg Prostate Cancer
Awareness Group
813-327-9337

Prostate Cancer Support Group Florida
Urological Institute
813-345-2274

Sarasota
Man-to-Man—
Sarasota/Bradenton/South Sarasota
American Cancer Society
941-365-2858

Satellite Beach
Man-to-Man Prostate Cancer Support
Group
407-777 0716

South Miami
Pan American Hospital Support
Group—Hispanic
305-444-2858

Sunrise
US TOO Prostate Cancer Support
Group—Sunrise
305-748-1633

Vero Beach
Vero Beach Prostate Cancer Support
Group
407-231-2463

West Palm Beach
Wellington Regional Medical Center
Support
561-686-4503

GEORGIA

Atlanta
Crawford Long Hospital
404 881-0966

Prostate Support Association (PSA) The
Emory Clinic
404-778-4335

US TOO Prostate Cancer Support
Group Grady Memorial Hospital
404-616-4466

Athens
Athens Area Prostate Cancer Support
Group
706-543-5602

ILLINOIS

Chicago
Northwestern Memorial Hospital
312-908-6880

Countryside
Loyola University Medical Center
Prostate Support
708-579-0819

Elmhurst
US TOO Prostate Cancer Support
Group Elmhurst Memorial Hospital
708-833-1400 x 2721

Glenview
US TOO Prostate Support Group
Glenbrook Hospital
847-657-5776

Harvey
Ingalls Hospital—US TOO
708-915-6193

Hinsdale
Hinsdale Hospital Prostate Cancer
Support Group
630-856-7526

Homewood
Homewood Cancer Center Men's
Group
708-798-9171

Kankakee
US TOO Prostate Cancer Support
Group
815-939-3190

Lake Forest
US TOO Prostate Cancer Support
Group Lake Forest Hospital
847-234-3300

Lombard
US TOO Prostate Cancer Support
Group
630-620-5850

Northbrook
US TOO—Highland Park Hospital
847-498-5413

Peoria
Affiliated Urology Specialists
309-655-7700

US TOO—Peoria Chapter
309-691-6523

Rockford
US TOO Prostate Cancer Support
Group Swedish American Hospital
815-968-4400 x 4315

Schaumburg
US TOO—Columbia Hoffman Estates
Medical Center
847-310-0939

INDIANA

Fort Wayne
Northeast Indiana Urology Prostate
Support Group
219-436-6667

Prostate Cancer Support Group
219-484-8340

US TOO Prostate Cancer Support
Group Cancer Services of Allen County
219-484-9560

IOWA

Cedar Rapids
US TOO Mercy Cancer Center Prostate
Support
319-398-6452

Davenport
Urological Associates Prostate Support
Group
319-359-1641

Des Moines
Iowa Methodist Prostate Cancer
Support Group John Stoddard Cancer
Center
515-241-4171

Iowa City
US TOO Prostate Cancer Support
Group Mercy Hospital
319-339-3662
319-338-6367

Waterloo
US TOO Prostate Cancer Support
Group Allen Hospital
319-235-5144

KANSAS

Wichita
US TOO Prostate Cancer Support
Group
316-687-4206

KENTUCKY

Lexington
University of Kentucky Medical Center
606-323-5649

LOUISIANA

Baton Rouge
Man-to-Man Support Group Mary
Perkins Cancer Treatment Center
504-767-0847

Shreveport
Louisiana State University Medical
Center
318-675-7771

MARYLAND

Annapolis
Prostate Cancer Support Group
Suburban Hospital
410-267-1511
301-530-3188

Baltimore
Man-to-Man Prostate Cancer Support
Group Good Samaritan Hospital
410-433-7300
410-931-6850

Prostate Cancer Networking Group The
Wellness Community
410-832-2719

US TOO Prostate Cancer Support
Group Greater Baltimore Medical
Center
410-828-2961

Bethesda
Prostate Cancer Support Group
301-229-3614

Clinton
Prostate Cancer Support Group
Southern Maryland Hospital
301-899-4658

Cordova
US TOO Prostate Cancer Support
Group
410-822-1000 x 5600

Edgewater
Prostate Cancer Support Group—
Annapolis
410-267-1509

Silver Spring
Prostate Support Group Walter Reed
Army Medical Center
301-384-5260
301-292-2587

Urinary Incontinence Support Group
for Prostate Cancer Survivors
202-761-0466

Suitland
Andrews Air Force Base Prostate
Support Group
301-967-0750

MAINE

Bangor
US TOO Prostate Cancer Support
Group
207-942-1284

Corinna
Prostate Support Group
207-368-5323

Northport
Prostate Support Group
207-338-5165

Portland
Prostate Cancer Support Group
207-773-6698

MASSACHUSETTS

Amesbury
Amesbury Health Center Prostate
Support Group
508-465-5361

Andover
Merrimack Valley Prostate Cancer
Support Group
508-475-6313 x 5401

Ayer
Nashoba Valley—US TOO
508-772-2789

Beverly
Beverly Hospital Prostate Cancer
Support Group
508-922-3000 x 2404
508-927-3747

Braintree
Prostate Cancer Support Group
617-843-2211

Brighton
Baystate Urology Prostate Cancer
Support Group
617-782-1200

Brockton
Prostate Cancer Support Group
508-587-3643

Brookline
Prostate Cancer Support Group
617-566-6761

Chelmsford
US TOO Prostate Support Group—
Lowell
508-256-8643

Dedham
Prostate Cancer Support Group
617-329-1400

Dorchester
Longwood Medical Area
617-288-7886

Hyannis
Prostate Cancer Support Group Cape
Cod Hospital
508-771-1800 x 2302
508-428-3612

Lowell
Lowell General Hospital Prostate
Support Group
508-937-6386

Lynn
Northshore Prostate Cancer Support
Group
617-599-3495

Northshore Prostate Cancer Support
Group
617-599-7791

Marshfield
Quincy Hospital Prostate Cancer
Support Group
617-834-2818

Medford
St. Elizabeth's Prostate Cancer Support
Group
617-396-4859

Millbury
Prostate Cancer Support Group
508-865-6733

Newburyport
Merrimack Valley Prostate Cancer
Support Group
508-462-8515

Newton
US TOO Prostate Support Group—
Newton/Wellesley
617-244-2421

Sharon
Prostate Cancer Support Group
617-784-2513

Somerville
Longwood Medical Area Prostate
Support Group
617-625-4875

Sunderland
Sunderland Prostate Cancer Support
Group
413-665-7741

Waltham
Prostate Cancer Support Group
617-893-1717

Waltham Prostate Cancer Support
Group Deaconess Waltham Hospital
617-647-6680

Wellesley
Prostate Cancer Support Group
617-431-7721

Wilbraham
Prostate Cancer Support Group of
Western Mass
413-599-1791

Winchester
Winchester Hospital Prostate Cancer
Support Group
617-729-0858

MICHIGAN
Ann Arbor
Prostate Cancer Support Group St.
Joseph Hospital
313-712-3655

Prostate Cancer Support Group
University Of Michigan
313-936-5938

Detroit
B.R.A.V.E. Prostate Support Group
Harper Hospital
313-745-9102

Man-to-Man Prostate Cancer Support
Group Providence Hospital
810-356-8870

Farmington Hills
Botsford Hospital
810-477-6100

Lansing
Prostate Cancer Support Group of Mid
Michigan Michigan State University
517-353-8828 x 3 or 6

Grand Rapids
The Survivors Association Grand
Clinical Oncology
616-391-1230
616-957-1943

Livonia
Livonia Area US TOO Prostate Cancer
Group
810-353-3060

Novi
Prostate Cancer Support Group
810-478-6811

Rochester
Roundtable Supporting Victims of
Prostate Cancer (RSVP)
810-651-4289

MINNESOTA
Edina
US TOO Prostate Cancer Support
Group Fairview Southdale Hospital
612-924-5714

Minneapolis
Mercy/Unity Hospital Prostate Cancer
Support Group
612-780-6707

MISSISSIPPI

Lucedale
US TOO Prostate Cancer Support
Group
601-947-3027

MISSOURI

Hannibal
Hannibal Regional Hospital—Prostate
Support Group
573-248-5188

Kansas City
US TOO Prostate Cancer Support
816-358-6036

The Cancer Institute
816-751-2929

St Louis
St. Louis Support Group
314-525-7636

US TOO Prostate Cancer Support
Group St. John's Mercy Cancer Center
314-569-6400

MONTANA

Billings
Man-to-Man Northern Rockies Cancer
Center
406-248-2212

NORTH CAROLINA

Asheville
US TOO Prostate Cancer Support
Group Life After Cancer
704-252-4106

Chapel Hill
Chapel Hill Prostate Cancer Support
Group University of North Carolina at
Chapel Hill
919-966-6686

Charlotte
US TOO Prostate Cancer Support
Group
704-384-5223

Durham
Duke Hospital Prostate Cancer Support
Group
919-684-6234

Newton
US TOO—Hickory
704-466-0064

Raleigh
Man-to-Man/US TOO/PAACT Prostate
Support Group
919-787-4819

Tryon
Person-to-Person Prostate Cancer
Support Group
704-859-2288

US TOO Prostate Cancer Support and
Educational Group
704-859-5647

Winston-Salem
US TOO—Forsyth Memorial Hospital
919-718-8181

NEBRASKA

Omaha
Man-to-Man Prostate Support Group
American Cancer Society
402-393-7742 x 0012

US TOO/Man-to-Man Prostate Cancer
Support Group
402-398-1348

US TOO Prostate Cancer Support
Group
402-821-3255

Manchester
Optima Health Center Prostate Support
603-623-7658

Prostate Cancer Group Elliot Hospital
603-628-4170

NEW JERSEY

Clifton
US TOO—Passaic General Hospital
Center at Passaic
201-779-7231

Elizabeth
Prostate Cancer Support Group
Elizabeth General
908-629-8175

Hackensack
Hackensack Medical Center— US TOO
Support Group Northern NJ Cancer
Center
201-996-5836

Hackettstown
St. Clare's Hospital Prostate Support—
Denville
201-989-3016

Jersey City
Christ Hospital Prostate Cancer Support
Group
201-795-8030

Lakehurst
Prostate Support Group
908-657-9829

Lawrenceville
NJ PAACT Support Group— Princeton
609-896-2516

Livingston
Prostate Cancer Support Group St.
Barnabas Medical Center
908-755-9411
201-533-5000 x 8414

Martinsville
Prostate Cancer Support Group
Columbia Presbyterian
212-536-0415

Miliville
Prostate Support Group South Jersey
Hospital
609-692-1364

Montclair
Prostate Support Group The
Mountainside Hospital
201-429-6128

Morristown
US TOO Prostate Cancer Support
Group Morristown Memorial Hospital
201-539-7812
201-895-2135
201-971-4063

Mount Laurel
Man-to-Man Prostate Support
Burlington County
609-273-0600

Neptune
US TOO—Jersey Shore Medical Center
908-775-5500
608-776-4633

New Brunswick
Prostate Cancer Support Group The
Cancer Institute of New Jersey
908-235-6781

Pamona
Prostate Cancer Support Group Atlantic
City Medical Center
609-652-3570

Passaic
US TOO Prostate Cancer Support
Group General Hospital at Passaic
201-777-5888

Red Bank
Riverview Hospital Prostate Support
Group
908-530-2468

Ridgewood
US TOO Prostate Cancer Support
Group Ridgewood Valley Hospital
201-447-8557

Somerville
Prostate Cancer Support Group—
Somerville Somerville Medical Center
908-704-3794

Trenton
Prostate Cancer Support Group—
Trenton Mercer Medical Center
609-394-4255

Vineland
Prostate Cancer Support Group—
Cumberland County
609-691-7296

Wayne
Packanack Lake Area Prostate Support
Group
201-696-6483

Whiting
Community Medical Center Support—
Toms River
908-240-8200
908-240-8207

NEW YORK

Amherst
Prostate Cancer Support Group
816-834-1713

Batavia
US TOO Prostate Cancer Support
Group
716-343-8314

Brooklyn
VA Medical Center Prostate Cancer
Support Group
718-836-6600 x 6366

Binghamton
US TOO Prostate Cancer Support
Group
607-797-1730

Buffalo
Prostate Cancer Support Group
716-835-0368

Cassadaga
US TOO Prostate Cancer Support
Group of Western NY
716-595-8749

Elmira
Falck Cancer Center Prostate Cancer
Support Group
800-262-3252

Kingston
Man-to-Man Prostate Cancer Support
Group
914-338-8005

Manhasset
US TOO Prostate Cancer Support
Group North Shore University
516-629-6188
516-926-4357

Middletown
US TOO Chapter—Middletown
914-343-7184

New York City
Columbia Presbyterian Medical Center
Support Group
212-305-2991

US TOO—NY Hospital/Cornell Medical
Center
212-746-5450

US TOO Prostate Cancer Support
Group Manhattan Memorial Sloan
Kettering Cancer Center
212-639-7036

Riverhead
US TOO Prostate Cancer Support
Group Riverhead Central Suffolk
Hospital
516-369-1228

Troy
Man-to-Man Capital District—Albany
518-274-5570

Wappingers Falls
Man-to-Man—Poughkeepsie ACS
914-452-2635

NEVADA

Henderson
Prostate Cancer Support Group
702-454-6226

Las Vegas
East Vegas Valley Prostate Cancer
Support Group
702-456-7591
702-435-4951

Southern Nevada US TOO Support
Group
702-870-3663

OHIO

Aurora
Portage County—US TOO Prostate
Cancer Support Group
216-562-8209

Cincinnati
Man-to-Man
513-791-4060

St. Luke Hospital
513-731-3346

Columbus
Riverside Urology Prostate Cancer
Support Group
614-262-6575
614-451-2141

Dayton
Man-to-Man Prostate Cancer Support
Group Franciscan Medical Center
513-229-7070

OREGON

Portland
Kaiser Permanente Prostate Cancer
Support Group
503-280-5057

Prostate Cancer Support Group Legacy
Good Samaritan Hospital
503-413-7711

PENNSYLVANIA

Byrn Mawr
Byrn Mawr Prostate Cancer Support
Group
610-526-3428

Drexel Hill
Prostate Cancer Support Group
Delaware County Memorial Hospital
610-284-8487

Greensburg
Westmoreland Regional Hospital
412-832-4090

Hershey
US TOO Support Group
717-531-8521

Lancaster
Pennsylvania PAACT
717-299-3227

Prostate Cancer Support Group of
Antelope Valley
805-945-0601

US TOO—Lancaster
717-786-1722

Philadelphia
Prostate Cancer Support Group Albert
Einstein Medical Center
215-456-3441

Prostate Support Group—For Men Only
Fox Chase Cancer Center
215-728-2668

Pittsburgh
Pittsburgh Cancer Institute
412-692-4724

Prostate Cancer Support Group
412-621-0248

Reading
US TOO Prostate Cancer Support
Group St. Joseph's Medical Center 610-
378-2543

Shillington
US TOO Prostate Cancer Support
Group 215-775-4205

RHODE ISLAND

East Providence
US TOO Prostate Support Group Roger
Williams Hospital
401-433-2133

Riverside
Prostate Cancer Support Group
401-433-2133

SOUTH CAROLINA

Charleston
Prostate Cancer Support Group Medical
University of South Carolina 803-792-
4531

Columbia
US TOO Prostate Cancer Support
Group 803-799-5288

Florence
US TOO Support Group Carolinas
Hospital System
803-661-4350

SOUTH DAKOTA

Rapid City
US TOO—Black Hills Area Chapter
605-343-8100

TENNESSEE

Bristol
Tenneva Prostate Cancer Support
Group
423-652-1811
423-968-1255

Cookeville
US TOO—Upper Cumberland Chapter
615-528-5547

TEXAS

Austin
US TOO Prostate Cancer Support
Group—Austin
512-836-8634

Dallas
Prostate Cancer Support Group
214-490-6253

Prostate Cancer Support Medical
City Dallas
214-661-4847

Prostate Cancer Support Group
Presbyterian Hospital
214-345-5290

US TOO—Methodist Hospital
214-947-2917

Denton
US TOO Prostate Cancer Support
Group
817-382-7516

Houston
Prostate Cancer Support Group Baylor
College of Medicine
713-552-1075

TEX US TOO—St. Luke's Methodist
Church
713-722-0208

US TOO Prostate Cancer Support
Group Houston Memorial Hospital
713-226-2273

Kerrville
US TOO Kerrville Texas Chapter
210-257-7533
210-367-4483
210-896-8792

Lubbock
US TOO—Man-to-Man Prostate Cancer
Support Group
806-792-3736

Odessa
Man-to-Man Prostate Cancer Support
Group West Texas Cancer Center
915-335-8275

Plano
US TOO North Dallas Prostate Cancer
Support Group
972-612-8037

Temple
Central Texas Prostate Cancer Support
Group Scott and White Cancer Center
817-724-1178

UTAH

Salt Lake City
Man-to-Man Prostate Cancer Support
Group McKay-De Hospital
801-625-6779

VIRGINIA

Alexandria
Alexandria Hospital US TOO Prostate
Support Group
301-405-3406

Falls Church
US TOO Fairfax Hospital Chapter Life
with Cancer
703-698-2841

Reston
Prostate Cancer Support Group
703-437-4079

Richmond
US TOO Richmond Chapter
804-378-9652

Virginia Beach
US TOO Prostate Cancer Support
Group Virginia Beach/Norfolk
757-474-1981

Waynesboro
US TOO of the Valley
540-949-7078

WASHINGTON

Bellevue
Prostate Cancer Support Group
206-746-3999

Bellingham
Bellingham Prostate Cancer US TOO
Support Group
360-715-4144

Eastsound
Man-to-Man Prostate Cancer Support
Group—N.W.
206-376-2490

WASHINGTON DC

Washington
George Washington Prostate Cancer
Support Group
410-757-3543

Humana Health Group—
Washington DC
202-872-7108

Walter Reed US TOO Prostate Support
Group
202-782-3166

WEST VIRGINIA

Charleston
Prostate Cancer Support Group
304-727-7084

Huntington
Prostate Cancer Support Group
304-529-1101

WISCONSIN

Green Bay
Green Bay/Brown County Prostate
Support Group
414-468-4820
414-336-1275

Milwaukee
Columbia Hospital Prostate Cancer
Support Group
414-961-7323

Prostate Cancer Support Group of
Wisconsin
414-527-3000

WYOMING

Sheridan
Prostate Cancer Support Group
307-672-1806

GLOSSARY OF PCa RELATED TERMS

ABDOMEN: the part of the body below the ribs and above the pelvic bone that contains organs like the intestines, the liver, the kidneys, the stomach, the bladder, and the prostate

ABLATION: reduction of; for example, in the management of prostate cancer, hormonal ablation means the use of hormonal techniques to reduce the spread of prostate cancer cells and cryoablation means the use of deep freezing techniques to reduce the number of live prostate and prostate cancer cells

ADENOCARCINOMA: a form of cancer that develops from a malignant abnormality in the cells lining a glandular organ such as the prostate; almost all prostate cancers are adenocarcinomas

ADJUVANT: an additional treatment used to increase the effectiveness of the primary therapy; radiation therapy and hormonal therapy are often used as adjuvant treatments following a radical prostatectomy

ADRENAL GLANDS: the two adrenal glands are located above the kidneys; they produce a variety of different hormones, including sex hormones – the adrenal androgens

ADRENALECTOMY: the surgical removal of one or both adrenal glands

AGE-ADJUSTED: modified to take account of the age of an individual or group of individuals; for example, prostate cancer survival data and average normal PSA values can be adjusted according to the ages of groups of men

ALKALINE PHOSPHATASE: an enzyme in blood, bone, kidney, spleen, and lungs; used to detect bone or liver metastasis

ALPHA-BLOCKERS: pharmaceutical that act on the prostate by relaxing certain types of muscle tissue; these pharmaceutical are often used in the treatment of BPH

ANALOG: a synthetic chemical or pharmaceutical that behaves very like a normal chemical in the body, e.g., LHRH analogs

ANANDRON: trade or brand name for nilutamide

ANDROCUR: trade name for cyproterone, and antiandrogen

ANDROGEN: a hormone which is responsible for male characteristics and the development and function of male sexual organs (e.g., testosterone) produced mainly by the testicles but also in the cortex of the adrenal glands

ANESTHETIC: a drug that produces general or local loss of physical sensations, particularly pain; a "spinal" is the injection of a local anesthetic into the area surrounding the spinal cord

ANEUPLOID: having an abnormal number of sets of chromosomes; for example, tetraploid means having two paired sets of chromosomes, which is twice as many as normal; aneuploid cancer cells tend not to respond well to hormone therapy (see also diploid)

ANGIOGENESIS: the formation of new blood vessels; a characteristic of tumors

ANTERIOR: the front; for example, the anterior of the prostate is the part of the prostate that faces forward

ANTIANDROGEN: a compound (usually a synthetic pharmaceutical) which blocks or otherwise interferes with the normal action of androgens at cellular receptor sites

ANTIANDROGEN WITHDRAWAL RESPONSE (AAWR): a decrease in PSA caused by the withdrawal of an antiandrogen such as Casodex or Flutamide after CHT begins to fail; occurs when there are PCa cells that have mutated to feed on the anti-androgen rather than T and DHT; withdrawal kills those cells.

ANTIBIOTIC: a pharmaceutical that can kill certain types of bacteria

ANTIBODY: protein produced by the immune system as a defense against an invading or "foreign" material or substance (an antigen);

for example, when you get a cold, your body produces antibodies to the cold virus

ANTICOAGULANT: a pharmaceutical that helps to stop the blood from clotting

ANTIGEN: "foreign" material introduced into the body (a virus or bacterium, for example) or other material which the immune system considers to be "foreign" because it is not part of the body's normal biology (e.g., prostate cancer cells)

ANUS: the opening of the rectum

APEX: the tip or bottom of the prostate, e.g., the part of the prostate farthest away from the bladder

ASPIRATION: the use of suction to remove fluid or tissue, usually through a fine needle (e.g., aspiration biopsy)

ASYMPTOMATIC: having no recognizable symptoms of a particular disorder

AUTOLOGOUS: one's own; for example, autologous blood is a patient's own blood which is removed prior to surgery in case a patient needs a transfusion during or after surgery

BASE: the base of the prostate is the wide part at the top of the prostate closest to the bladder

BENIGN: relatively harmless; not cancerous; not malignant

BENIGN PROSTATIC HYPERPLASIA (or HYPERTROPHY) (BPH): A noncancerous condition of the prostate that results in the growth of both glandular and stromal (supporting connective) tumorous tissue, enlarging the prostate and obstructing urination (see prostatitis)

BENIGN PROSTATIC HYPERTROPHY (BPH): similar to benign prostatic hyperplasia, but caused by an increase in the size of cells rather than the growth of more cells

BICALUTAMIDE: a nonsteroidal antiandrogen available in the USA and some European countries for the treatment of advanced prostate cancer

BILATERAL: both sides; for example, a bilateral orchiectomy is an orchiectomy in which both testicles are removed and a bilateral adrenalectomy is an operation in which both adrenal glands are removed

BIOPSY: sampling of tissue from a particular part of the body (e.g., the prostate) in order to check for abnormalities such as cancer; in the case of prostate cancer, biopsies are usually carried out under ultrasound guidance using a specially designed device known as a prostate biopsy gun; removed tissue is typically examined microscopically by a pathologist in order to make a precise diagnosis of the patient's condition

BLADDER: the hollow organ in which urine is collected and stored in the body

BLOOD CHEMISTRY: measured concentrations of many chemicals in the blood; abnormal values can indicate spread of cancer or side effects of therapy

BLOOD COUNT: analysis of blood cells and platelets; abnormal values can indicate cancer in the bone or side effects of therapy

BONE MARROW: soft tissue in bone cavities that produces blood cells

BONE SCAN: a technique more sensitive than conventional x-rays which uses a radiolabeled agent to identify abnormal or cancerous growths within or attached to bone; in the case of prostate cancer, a bone scan is used to identify bony metastases which are definitive for cancer which has escaped from the prostate; metastases appear as "hot spots" on the film; however the absence of hot spots does not prove the absence of tiny metastases

BOWEL PREPARATION: the cleaning of the bowels or intestines which is normal prior to abdominal surgery such as radical prostatectomy

BPH: see BENIGN PROSTATIC HYPERPLASIA

BRACHYTHERAPY: A form of radiation therapy in which radioactive seeds or pellets which emit radiation are implanted in order to kill surrounding tissue (e.g., the prostate, including prostate cancer cells)

CAB: COMPLETE ANDROGEN BLOCKADE (see CHT)

CANCER: the growth of abnormal cells in the body in an uncontrolled manner; unlike benign tumors, these tend to invade surrounding tissues, and spread to distant sites of the body via the blood stream and lymphatic system

CAPSULE: the fibrous tissue which acts as an outer lining of the prostate

CARCINOMA: a form of cancer that originates in tissues which line or cover a particular organ; See ADENOCARCINOMA

CASODEX: brand or trade name of bicalutamide in the USA

CASTRATION: the use of surgical or medical techniques to eliminate testosterone produced by the testes

CAT SCAN: COMPUTERIZED AXIAL TOMOGRAPHY (also CT) is a method of combining images from multiple x-rays under the control of a computer to produce cross sectional or three-dimensional pictures of the internal organs which can be used to identify abnormalities; the CAT scan can identify prostate enlargement but is not always effective for assessing the stage of prostate cancer; for evaluating metastases of the lymph nodes or more distant soft tissue sites, the s is significantly more accurate

CATHETER: a hollow (usually flexible plastic) tube which can be used to drain fluids from or inject fluids into the body; in the case of prostate cancer, it is common for patients to have a transurethral catheter to drain urine for some time after treatment by surgery or some forms of radiation therapy

CDUS: COLOR-FLOW DOPPLER ULTRASOUND; an ultrasound method that more clearly images tumors by observing the

Doppler shift in sound waves caused by the rapid flow of blood through tiny blood vessels that are characteristic of tumors

CGA: chromogranin A; a small cell prostate cancer or neuroendocrine cell marker

CHEMOPREVENTION: the use of a pharmaceutical or other substance to prevent the development of cancer

CHEMOTHERAPY: the use of pharmaceutical or other chemicals to kill cancer cells; in many cases chemotherapeutic agents kill not only cancer cells but also other cells in the body, which makes such agents potentially very dangerous

CHT: COMBINED HORMONAL THERAPY: the use of more than one hormone in therapy; especially the use of LHRH analogs (e.g., Lupron, Zoladex) to block the production of testosterone by the testes, plus antiandrogens (e.g., Casodex (bicalutamide), Eulexin (flutamide), Anadron (nilutamide), Androcur (cyproterone))) to compete with DHT for cell sites thereby depriving cancer cells of DHT needed for growth

CLINICAL TRIAL: a carefully planned experiment to evaluate a treatment or a medication (often a new pharmaceutical) for an unproven use; Phase I trials are very preliminary short-term trials involving a few patients to see if drugs have any activity or any serious side effects; Phase II trials may involve 20 to 50 patients and are designed to estimate the most active dose of a new drug and determine its side effects; Phase III trials involve many patients and compare a new therapy against the current standard or best available therapy

COMBINATION THERAPY: see CHT

COMPLICATION: an unexpected or unwanted effect of a treatment, pharmaceutical, or other procedure

CONFORMATIONAL THERAPY: the use of careful planning and delivery techniques designed to focus radiation on the areas of the prostate and surrounding tissue which need treatment and protect areas which do not need treatment; three-dimensional conformational therapy is a more sophisticated form of this method

CONTRACTURE: scarring which can occur at the bladder neck after a radical prostatectomy and which results in narrowing of the passage between the bladder and the urethra

CORPORA CAVERNOSA: a part of a man's penis which fills with blood when he is sexually excited, giving the organ the stiffness required for intercourse

CORPORA SPONGIOSUM: a spongy chamber in a man's penis which fills with blood when he is sexually excited, giving the organ the stiffness required for intercourse

CRYOABLATION: see cryosurgery

CRYOSURGERY: the use of liquid nitrogen probes to freeze a particular organ to extremely low temperatures to kill the tissue, including any cancerous tissue; When used to treat prostate cancer, the cryoprobes are guided by transrectal ultrasound

CRYOTHERAPY: see cryosurgery

CT SCAN: COMPUTERIZED or COMPUTED TOMOGRAPHY; See CATSCAN

CYPROTERONE: an antiandrogen

CYSTOSCOPE: an instrument used by physicians to look inside the bladder and the urethra

CYSTOSCOPY: the use of a cystoscope to look inside the bladder and the urethra

CYTOKINES: growth factors important to cellular function

DEBULKING: reduction of the volume of cancer by one of several techniques; most frequently used to imply surgical debulking

DES: see diethylstilbestrol

DHT: see dihydrotestosterone

DIAGNOSIS: the evaluation of signs, symptoms, and selected test results by a physician to determine the physical and biological causes of the signs and symptoms and whether a specific disease or disorder is involved

DIETHYLSTILBESTROL: a female hormone commonly used in the 1960s and 1970s for treatment of prostate cancer

DIGITAL RECTAL EXAMINATION: the use by a physician of a lubricated and gloved finger inserted into the rectum to feel for abnormalities of the prostate and rectum

DIHYDROTESTOSTERONE: (DHT) (5 alpha-dihydrotestosterone) the male hormone which is most active in the prostate; it is made when an enzyme (5 alpha reductase) in the prostate stimulates the transformation of testosterone to DHT

DIFFERENTIATION: the use of the differences between prostate cancer cells when seen under the microscope as a method to grade the severity of the disease; well differentiated cells are easily recognized as normal cells, while poorly differentiated cells are abnormal, cancerous and difficult to recognize as belonging to any particular type of cell group

DIPLOID: having one complete set of normally paired chromosomes, i.e., a normal amount of DNA; diploid cancer cells tend to grow slowly and respond well to hormone therapy

DNA: DEOXYRIBONUCLEIC ACID; the basic biologically active chemical which defines the physical development and growth of nearly all living organisms

DOUBLE-BLIND: a form of clinical trial in which neither the physician nor the patient knows the actual treatment which any individual patient is receiving; double-blind trials are a way of minimizing the effects of the personal opinions of patients and physicians on the results of the trial

DOUBLING TIME: the time that it takes a particular focus of cancer to double in size

DOWNSIZING: the use of hormonal or other forms of management to reduce the volume of prostate cancer in and/or around the prostate prior to attempted curative treatment

DOWNSTAGING: the use of hormonal or other forms of management in the attempt to lower the clinical stage of prostate cancer prior to attempted curative treatment (e.g., from stage T3a to stage T2b); this technique is highly controversial

DRE: see digital rectal examination

DYSPLASIA: see PIN

DYSURIA: urination which is problematic or painful

EDEMA: swelling or accumulation of fluid in some part of the body

EJACULATORY DUCTS: The tubular passages through which semen reaches the prostatic urethra during orgasm

ERECTILE DYSFUNCTION: See IMPOTENCE

EMCYT: the brand or trade name of estramustine phosphate in the USA

ENDOGENOUS: inherent naturally to the organism

ESTRAMUSTINE PHOSPHATE: a chemotherapeutic agent used in the treatment of some patients with late stage prostate cancer

ESTROGEN: a female hormone; certain estrogens (e.g., diethyl-stilbestrol) are used by some physicians in treatment on prostate cancer

EULEXIN: the brand or trade name of flutamide in the USA

EXPERIMENTAL: an unproven (or even untested) technique or procedure; not that certain experimental treatments are commonly used in the management of prostate cancer

EXTERNAL RADIATION THERAPY (also EXTERNAL BEAM THERAPY): a form of radiation therapy in which the radiation is delivered by a machine pointed at the area to be radiated

FALSE NEGATIVE: an erroneous negative test result; for example, an imaging test that fails to show the presence of a cancer tumor later found by biopsy to be present in the patient is said to have returned false negative result

FALSE POSITIVE: a positive test result mistakenly identifying a state or condition that does not in fact exist

FINASTERIDE: an inhibitor of the enzyme (5 alpha-reductase) that stimulates the conversion of testosterone to DHT; used to treat BPH

FLARE REACTION: a temporary increase in tumor growth and symptoms caused by LHRH agonists; can be mild to dangerous; may be prevented by taking an antiandrogen (Casodex) several days before starting LHRH agonist (Lupron or Zoladex)

FLOW CYTOMETRY: a measurement method that determines the fraction of cells that are diploid, tetraploid, aneuploid, etc.

FLUTAMIDE: an antiandrogen used in the palliative hormonal treatment of advanced prostate cancer and sometimes in the adjuvant and neoadjuvant hormonal treatment of earlier stages of prostate cancer; normal dosage is 2 capsules every 8 hours (not just at meals)

FREQUENCY: the need to urinate often

FROZEN SECTION: a technique in which removed tissue is frozen, cut into thin slices, and stained for microscopic examination; a pathologist can rapidly complete a frozen section analysis, and for this reason, it is commonly used during surgery to quickly provide the surgeon with vital information such as a preliminary pathologic opinion of the presence or absence of prostate cancer (usually in the pelvic lymph nodes)

GASTROINTESTINAL: related to the digestive system and/or the intestines

GENITAL SYSTEM: the biological system which, in males, includes the testicles, the vas deferens, the prostate, and the penis

GENITOURINARY SYSTEM: the combined genital and urinary systems; also known as the genitourinary tract

GLAND: a structure or organ which produces a substance which is used in another part of the body

GLEASON: name of physician who developed the Gleason grading system commonly used to grade prostate cancer

GLEASON SCORE: a widely used method for classifying the cellular differentiation of cancerous tissues; the less the cancerous cells appear like normal cells, the more malignant the cancer; two numbers, each from 1-5, are assigned successively to the two most predominant patterns of differentiation present in the examined tissue sample and are added together to produce the Gleason score; high numbers indicate poor differentiation and therefore cancer

GNRH - genadotropin-releasing hormone, see LHRH ANALOGS

GOSERELIN ACETATE: a luteinizing hormone releasing hormone analog used in the palliative hormonal treatment of advanced prostate cancer and sometimes in the adjuvant and neoadjuvant hormonal treatment of earlier stages of prostate cancer

GRADE: a means of describing the potential degree of severity of a cancer based on the appearance of cancer cells under a microscope; see also Gleason Score

GYNECOMASTIA: enlargement or tenderness of the male breasts or nipples; a possible side effect of hormonal therapy

HEMATOSPERMIA: the occurrence of blood in the semen

HEMATURIA: the occurrence of blood in the urine

HEREDITY: the historical distribution of biological characteristics through a group of related individuals via their DNA

HEREDITARY: inherited from one's parents and earlier generations

HISTOLOGY: the study of the appearance and behavior of tissue, usually carried out under a microscope by a pathologist (who is a physician) or a histologist (who is not necessarily a physician)

HORMONE: biologically active chemicals that are responsible for the development of secondary sexual characteristics

HORMONE THERAPY: the use of hormones, hormone analogs, and certain surgical techniques to treat disease (in this case advanced prostate cancer) either on their own or in combination with other hormones or in combination with other methods of treatment; because prostate cancer is usually dependent on male hormones to grow, hormonal therapy can be an effective means of alleviating symptoms and retarding the development of the disease

HOT FLASH: the sudden sensation of warmth in the face, neck and upper body; a side effect of many forms of hormone therapy

HYPERCALCEMIA: abnormally high concentrations of calcium in the blood, indicating leeching of calcium from bone (tumors raise serum calcium levels by destroying bone or by releasing PTH or a PTH-like substance, osteoclastactivating factor, prostaglandins, and perhaps, a vitamin D-like sterol). Symptoms of hypercalcemia may include drowsiness, lethargy, headaches, depression or apathy, irritability, confusion; weakness, muscle flaccidity, bone pain, pathologic fractures; signs of heart block, cardiac arrest in systole, hypertension; anorexia, nausea, vomiting, constipation, dehydration, polydipsia; renal polyuria, flank pain, and eventually, azotemia (excess of urea or other nitrogenous substances in the blood).

HYPERPLASIA: enlargement of an organ or tissue because of an increase in the number of cells in that organ or tissue; see also BPH

HYPERTHERMIA: treatment that uses heat; for example heat produced by microwave radiation

IMAGING: a technique or method allowing a physician to see something which would not normally be visible

IMMUNE SYSTEM: the biological system which protects a person or animal from the effects of foreign materials such as bacteria, viruses, cancer cells, and other things which might make that person or animal sick

IMPLANT: a device that is inserted into the body; e.g., a tiny container of radioactive material inserted in or near a tumor; also a device inserted in order to replace or substitute for an ability which has been lost; for example, a penile implant is a device which can be surgically inserted into the penis to provide rigidity for intercourse

IMPOTENCE: the inability to have or to maintain an erection

INCIDENTAL: insignificant or irrelevant; for example, incidental prostate cancer (also known as latent prostate cancer) is a form of prostate cancer which is of no clinical significance to the patient in whom it is discovered

INCONTINENCE: (urinary incontinence) loss of urinary control; there are various kinds and degrees of incontinence; overflow incontinence is a condition in which the bladder retains urine after voiding; as a consequence, the bladder remains full most of the time, resulting in involuntary seepage of urine from the bladder, stress incontinence is the involuntary discharge of urine when there is increased pressure upon the bladder, as in coughing or straining to lift heavy objects; total incontinence is the inability to voluntarily exercise control over the sphincters of the bladder neck and urethra, resulting in total loss of retentive ability

INDICATION: a reason for doing something or taking some action; also used to mean the approved clinical application of a pharmaceutical

INFLAMMATION: any form of swelling or pain or irritation

INFORMED CONSENT: permission to proceed given by a patient after being fully informed of the purposes and potential consequences of a medical procedure

INTERFERON: a body protein that affects antibody production and can modulate (regulate) the immune system

INTERLEUKIN: a blood protein that helps fight infection and cancer

INTERSTITIAL: within a particular organ; for example, interstitial prostate radiation therapy is radiation therapy applied within the prostate using implanted radioactive pellets or seeds (see also brachytherapy)

INTRAVENOUS: into a vein

INVASIVE: requiring an incision or the insertion of an instrument or substance into the body

INVESTIGATIONAL: a drug or procedure allowed by the FDA for use in clinical trials

IVP: INTRAVENOUS PYELOGRAM; a procedure which introduces an X-ray absorbing dye into the urinary tract in order to allow the physician a superior image of the tract by taking an X-ray; used to check for the spread of cancer to the kidneys and bladder

KEGEL EXERCISES: a set of exercises designed to improve the strength of the muscles used in urinating

KIDNEY: one of a pair of organs whose primary function is to filter the fluids passing through the body

LAPAROSCOPY: a technique which allows the physician to observe internal organs directly through a piece of optical equipment inserted directly into the body through a small surgical incision

LATENT: insignificant or irrelevant; for example, latent prostate cancer (also known as incidental prostate cancer) is a form of prostate cancer which is of no clinical significance to the patient in whom it is discovered

LEUPROLIDE ACETATE: a LHRH analog

LHRH: see luteinizing hormone releasing hormone

LHRH ANALOGS (or AGONISTS): Synthetic compounds that are chemically similar to Luteinizing Hormone Releasing Hormone (LHRH), but are sufficiently different that they suppress testicular production of testosterone by binding to the LHRH receptor in the pituitary gland and either have no biological activity and therefore competitively inhibits the action of LHRH, or has LHRH activity that exhausts the production of LH by the pituitary; used in the palliative hormonal treatment of advanced prostate cancer and sometimes in the adjuvant and neoadjuvant hormonal treatment of earlier stages of prostate cancer

LIBIDO: interest in sexual activity

LNCap: a line of human prostate cancer cells used in laboratory studies

LOBE: one of the two sides of an organ which clearly has two sides (e.g., the prostate or the brain)

LOCALIZED: restricted to a well defined area

LUPRON: the USA trade or brand name of leuprolide acetate, a LHRH agonist

LUTEINIZING HORMONE RELEASING HORMONE: a hormone responsible for stimulating the production of testosterone in the body

LYMPH (also LYMPHATIC FLUID): the clear fluid in which all of the cells in the body are constantly bathed; carries cells that help fight infection

LYMPH NODES: the small glands which occur throughout the body and which filter the clear fluid known as lymph or lymphatic fluid; lymph nodes filter out bacteria and other toxins, as well as cancer cells

LYMPHADENECTOMY Also knows as a pelvic lymph node dissection, this procedure involves the removal and microscopic examination of selected lymph nodes, a common site of metastatic disease with prostate cancer; this procedure can be performed during surgery prior to the removal of the prostate gland, or by means of a small incision a "laparoscopic lymphadenectomy" may be performed, a simple operation requiring only an overnight stay in the hospital

LYMPHATIC SYSTEM: the tissue and organs that produce, store and carry cells that fight infection; includes bone marrow, spleen, thymus, lymph nodes, and channels that carry lymph fluid

MAB: MAXIMAL ANDROGEN BLOCKADE (see CHT)

MAD: MAXIMAL ANDROGEN DEPRIVATION (see CHT)

MAGNETIC RESONANCE: absorption of specific frequencies of radio and microwave radiation by atoms placed in a strong magnetic field

MAGNETIC RESONANCE IMAGING (MRI): the use of magnetic resonance with atoms in body tissues to produce distinct cross-sectional, and even three-dimensional images of internal organs; MRI is primarily of use in staging biopsy-proven prostate cancer

MALIGNANCY: a growth or tumor composed of cancerous cells

MALIGNANT: cancerous; tending to become progressively worse and to result in death; having the invasive and metastatic (spreading) properties of cancer

MARGIN: normally used to mean the "surgical margin," which is the outer edge of the tissue removed during surgery; if the surgical margin shows no sign of cancer ("negative margins"), then the prognosis is good

MEDICAL ONCOLOGIST: an oncologist primarily trained in the use of medicines (rather than surgery) to treat cancer

METASTASIS: (plural is METASTASES) a secondary tumor formed as a result of a cancer cell or cells from the primary tumor site (e.g., the prostate) traveling through the body to a new site and then growing there

METASTASIZE: spread of a malignant tumor to other parts of the body

METASTATIC: having the characteristics of a secondary tumor

METASTATIC WORK UP: a group of tests, including bone scans, x-rays, and blood tests, to ascertain whether cancer has metastasized

METASTRON: the brand or trade name of strontium-89 in the US

MISSTAGING: the assignment of an incorrect clinical stage at initial diagnosis because of the difficulty of assessing the available information with accuracy

MONOCLONAL: formed from a single group of identical cells

MRI: see MAGNETIC RESONANCE IMAGING

MORBIDITY: unhealthy consequences and complications resulting from treatment

NEGATIVE: the term used to describe a test result which does not show the presence of the substance or material for which the test was carried out; for example, a negative bone scan would show no sign of bone metastases

NEOADJUVANT: added before; for example, neoadjuvant hormone therapy is hormone therapy given prior to another form of treatment such as a radical prostatectomy

NEOPLASIA: the growth of cells under conditions that would tend to prevent the development of normal tissue (e.g., a cancer)

NERVE SPARING: term used to describe a type of prostatectomy in which the surgeon saves the nerves that affect sexual and related functions

NILUTAMIDE: an antiandrogen, still experimental in the USA, but available in Canada and some other countries

NOCTURIA: the need to urinate frequently at night

NONINVASIVE: not requiring any incision or the insertion of an instrument or substance into the body

NSE: neuron-specific enolase; a neuroendocrine marker (see CGA)

ONCOLOGIST: a physician who specializes in the treatment of various types of cancer

ONCOLOGY: the branch of medical science dealing with tumors; an oncologist is a specialists in the study of cancerous tumors

ORCHIECTOMY: the surgical removal of the testicles

ORGAN: a group of tissues that work in concert to carry out a specific set of functions (e.g., the heart or the lungs or the prostate)

OSTEOBLAST: cell that forms bone

OSTEOCLAST: cell that breaks down bone-cell grows in bone tissue and apparently absorbs bone tissue, Pac-man fashion

OSTEOLYSIS: destruction of bone

OVERSTAGING: the assignment of an overly high clinical stage at initial diagnosis because of the difficulty of assessing the available information with accuracy (e.g., stage T3b as opposed to stage T2b)

PALLIATIVE: designed to relieve a particular problem without necessarily solving it; for example, palliative therapy is given in order to relieve symptoms and improve quality of life, but does not cure the patient

PALPABLE: capable of being felt during a physical examination by an experienced physician; in the case of prostate cancer, this normally refers to some form of abnormality of the prostate which can be felt during a digital rectal examination

PAP: PROSTATIC ACID PHOSPHATASE; an enzyme now measured only rarely to decide whether prostate cancer has escaped from the prostate

PATHOLOGIST: a physician who specializes in the examination of tissues and blood samples to help decide what diseases are present and therefore how they should be treated physicians data query; a NCI supported database available to physicians, containing current information on standard treatments and ongoing clinical trials

PDQ: physician data query; a NCI supported database available to physicians, containing current information on standard treatments and ongoing clinical trials

PELVIS: that part of the skeleton that joins the lower limbs of the body together

PENILE: of the penis

PENIS: the male organ used in urination and intercourse

PERINEAL: of the perineum

PERINEUM: the area of the body between the scrotum and the rectum; a perineal procedure uses this area as the point of entry into the body

PERIPHERAL: outside the central region

PIN: prostatic intraepitnelial (or intraductal) neoplasia; a pathologically identifiable condition believed to be a possible precursor of prostate cancer; also known more simply as dysplasia by many physicians

PLACEBO: a form of safe but non-active treatment frequently used as a basis for comparison with pharmaceutical in research studies

PLOIDY: a term used to describe the number of sets of chromosomes in a cell; see also diploid and aneuploid

POSITIVE: the term used to describe a test result which shows the presence of the substance or material for which the test was carried out; for example, a positive bone scan would show signs of bone metastases

POSTERIOR: the rear; for example, the posterior of the prostate is the part of the prostate that faces a man's back

PROGNOSIS: the patient's potential clinical outlook based on the status and probable course of his disease; chance of recovery

PROGRESSION: continuing growth or regrowth of the cancer

PROLACTIN: (PRL) a trophic hormone produced by the pituitary that increases androgen receptors, increases sensitivity to androgens, & regulates production & secretion of citrate

PROSCAR: brand name of finasteride

PROSTASCINT: a monoclonal antibody test directed against the prostate specific membrane antigen (PSMA); seems to focus on androgen independent tumor tissue

PROSTATE: the gland surrounding the urethra and immediately below the bladder in males

PROSTATECTOMY: surgical removal of part or all of the prostate gland

PROSTATE-SPECIFIC ANTIGEN: see PSA

PROSTATIC ACID PHOSPHATASE: see PAP

PROSTATITIS: infection or inflammation of the prostate gland treatable by medication and/or manipulation; (BPH is a more permanent laying down of fibroblasts and connective tissue caused when the prostate tries to contain a relatively silent chronic lower-grade infection, often requiring a TURP to relieve the symptoms)

PROSTHESIS: a man-made device used to replace a normal part or body function

PROTOCOL: a precise set of methods by which a research study is to be carried out

PSA: PROSTATE-SPECIFIC ANTIGEN; a protein secreted by the epithelial cells of the prostate gland including cancer cells; an elevated level in the blood indicates an abnormal condition of the prostate gland, either benign or malignant; it is used to detect potential problems in the prostate gland and to follow the progress of Pca therapy (see SCREENING)

PSA-II: prostate-specific antigen type II assay; reports the percentage of free-PSA to total-PSA (total-PSA = free PSA + bound-PSA); helpful for screening purposes when PSA values are above the normal threshold for an age group and less than 10; one study showed that men with PSA II > 25% had no PCa; those with <10% were likely to have PCa; not yet FDA approved (4/96), but available.

PSA RT-PCR: PSA reverse transcriptase-polymerase chain reaction; a blood test that detects micrometastatic cells circulating in the blood stream; may be useful as a screening tool to help avoid unnecessary invasive treatments (RP, RT, etc.) on patients with metastasized PCa; not FDA approved (4/96), but available at locations where FDA approved clinical trials of the test are being done.

PSM: prostate specific membrane; a membrane that surrounds the protoplasm (cytoplasm) of prostate cells

PSMA: prostate specific membrane antigen

QUALITY OF LIFE: an evaluation of health status relative to the patient's age, expectations, and physical and mental capabilities

RADIATION ONCOLOGIST: a physician who has received special training regarding the treatment of cancers with different types of radiation

RADIATION THERAPY (RT): the use of x-rays and other forms of radiation to destroy malignant cells and tissue

RADICAL: (in a surgical sense) directed at the cause of a disease; thus, radical prostatectomy is the surgical removal of the prostate with the intent to cure the problem believed to be caused by or within the prostate

RADICAL PROSTATECTOMY: an operation to remove the entire prostate gland and seminal vesicles

RADIOISOTOPE: a type of atom (or a chemical which is made with a type of atom) which emits radioactivity

RADIO SENSITIVITY: the degree to which a type of cancer responds to radiation therapy

RADIOTHERAPY: see RADIATION THERAPY

RANDOMIZED: the process of assigning patients to different forms of treatment in a research study in a random manner

RECTAL EXAM: see DIGITAL RECTAL EXAM

RECTUM: the final part of the intestines which ends at the anus

RECURRENCE: the reappearance of disease

REFRACTORY: resistant to therapy; e.g., hormone refractory prostate cancer is resistant to forms of treatment based on the use of hormones

REGRESSION: reduction in the size of a single tumor or reduction in the number and/or size of several tumors

REMISSION: the real or apparent disappearance of some or all or the signs and symptoms of cancer; the period (temporary or permanent) during which a disease remains under control, without progressing; even complete remission does not necessarily indicate cure

RESECTION: surgical removal

RESECTOSCOPE: instrument inserted through the urethra and used by a urologist to cut out tissue (usually from the prostate) while the physician can actually see precisely where he is cutting

RESISTANCE: (in a medical sense) ability to fight off a disease as a result of the effectiveness of the patient's immune system

RESPONSE: a decrease in disease that occurs because of treatment

RETENTION: difficulty in initiation of urination or the inability to completely empty the bladder

RETROPUBIC PROSTATECTOMY: surgical removal of the prostate through an incision in the abdomen

RISK: chance or probability that an event will or will not happen

RP: see RADICAL PROSTATECTOMY

RTPCR: see RT-PCR

RT-PCR: reverse transcriptase polymerase chain reaction; a technique which allows a physician to search for tiny quantities of a protein, such as PSA, in the blood or other body fluids and tissues; see PSA RT-PCR

SALVAGE: a procedure intended to "rescue" a patient following the failure of a prior treatment; for example, a salvage prostatectomy would be the surgical removal of the prostate after the failure of prior radiation therapy or cryosurgery

SCROTUM: the pouch of skin containing a man's testicles

SCREENING: to separate patients with tumors from those without tumors; multiple criteria are often used; the following PSA screening "cutoff" levels for PCa are replacing the older 4.0 value:

Age	PSA "cutoff"
40-49	2.5 ng/ml
50-59	3.5
60-69	4.5
70-79	6.5

SECONDARY TO: derived from or consequent to a primary event or thing

SELENIUM: a relatively rare nonmetallic element found in food in small quantities which may have some effect in prevention of cancer

SEMEN: the whitish, opaque fluid emitted by a male at ejaculation

SEMINAL: related to the semen; for example, the seminal vesicles are glands at the base of the bladder and connected to the prostate that provide nutrients for the semen

SENSITIVITY: the probability that a diagnostic test can correctly identify the presence of a particular disease assuming the proper conduct of the test; specifically, the number of true positive results divided by the sum of the true positive results and the false negative results; see SPECIFICITY

SEXTANT: having six parts; thus, a sextant biopsy is a biopsy that takes six samples

SIDE EFFECT: a reaction to a medication or treatment (most commonly used to mean an unnecessary or undesirable effect)

SIGN: physical changes which can be observed as a consequence of an illness or disease

SPECIFICITY: the probability that a diagnostic test can correctly identify the absence of a particular disease assuming the proper conduct of the test; specifically, the number of true negative results divided by the sum of the true negative results and the false positive results; a method that detects 95% of true PCa cases is highly sensitive, but if it also falsely indicates that 40% of those who do not have PCa do have PCa then its specificity is 60%, rather poor

STAGE: a term used to define the size and physical extent of a cancer

STAGING: the process of assigning a stage to a particular cancer in a specific patient in light of all the available information; it is used to help determine appropriate therapy; there are two staging methods: the Whitmore-Jewett staging classification (1956) and the more detailed TNM (tumor, nodes, metastases) classification (1992) of the American Joint Committee on Cancer and the International Union Against Cancer. Stage A (Whitmore-Jewett) becomes T1 (TNM) Stage B becomes T2 Stage C becomes T3

Whitmore-Jewett stages:
Stage A is clinically undetectable tumor confined to the gland and is an incidental finding at prostate surgery.
A1: well-differentiated with focal involvement
A2: moderately or poorly differentiated or involves multiple foci in the gland

Stage B is tumor confined to the prostate gland.
B0: nonpalpable. PSA-detected
B1: single nodule in one lobe of the prostate
B2: more extensive involvement of one lobe or involvement of both lobes

Stage C is a tumor clinically localized to the periprostatic area but extending through the prostatic capsule; seminal vesicles may be involved.
C1: clinical extracapsular extension
C2: extracapsular tumor producing bladder outlet or urethral obstruction

Stage D is metastatic disease.
D0: clinically localized disease (prostate only) but persistently elevated enzymatic serum acid phosphatase
D1: regional lymph nodes only
D2: distant lymph nodes, metastases to bone or visceral organs
D3: D2 prostate cancer patients who relapse after adequate endocrine therapy

TNM stages:
Primary Tumor (T)
TX: Primary tumor cannot be assessed
T0: No evidence of primary tumor

T1: Clinically inapparent tumor not palpable or visible by imaging

T1a: clinically inapparent tumor not palpable or visible by imaging

T1b:Tumor incidental histologic finding in more than 5% of tissue resected

T1c:Tumor identified by needle biopsy (e.g., because of elevated PSA)

T2:Tumor confined within the prostate

T2a:Tumor involves half of a lobe or less

T2b:Tumor involves more than half a lobe, but not both lobes

T2c:Tumor involves both lobes

T3:Tumor extends through the prostatic capsule

T3a: Unilateral extracapsular extension

T3b: Bilateral extracapsular extension

T3c:Tumor invades the seminal vesicle(s)

T4:Tumor is fixed or invades adjacent structures other than the seminal vesicles

T4a:Tumor invades any of bladder neck, external sphincter, or rectum

T4b:Tumor invades levator muscles and/or is fixed to the pelvic wall

Regional Lymph Nodes (N)

NX: Regional lymph nodes cannot be assessed

N0: No regional lymph nodes metastasis

N1: Metastasis in a single in greatest dimension

N2: Metastasis in a single 2 cm but not more than dimension; or multiple none more than 5 cm in lymph node, 2 cm or less lymph node, more than 5 cm in greatest lymph node metastases, greatest dimension

N3: Metastasis in a lymph node more than 5 cm in greatest dimension

Distant Metastases (M)

MX: Presence of distant metastasis cannot be assessed

M0: No distant metastasis

M1: Distant metastasis

Mla: Non-regional lymph node(s)
Mlb: Bone(s) Mlc: Other site(s)

STENT: a tube used by a surgeon to drain fluids

STRICTURE: scarring as a result of a procedure or an injury that constricts the flow of a fluid; for example, a urethral stricture would restrict the flow of urine through the urethra

STRONTIUM-89: an injectable radioactive product which is used to relieve bone pain in some patients with prostate cancer which no longer responds to hormones or appropriate forms of chemotherapy

SUBCAPSULAR: under the capsule; for example, a subcapsular orchiectomy is a form of castration in which the contents of each testicle is removed but the testicular capsules are then closed and remain in the scrotum

SUTURE: surgical stitching used in the closure of a cut or incision

SYMPTOM: a feeling, sensation, or experience associated with or resulting from a physical or mental disorder and noticeable by the patient

SYSTEMIC: throughout the whole body

TESTIS: one of two male reproductive glands located inside the scrotum which are the primary sources of the male hormone testosterone

TESTICLE: see testis

TESTOSTERONE (T): the male hormone or androgen which comprises most of the androgens in a man's body; chiefly produced by the testicles; may be produced in tissues from precursors such as androstenedione; T is essential to complete male sexual function and fertility

THERAPY: the treatment of disease or disability

TNM (tumor, nodes, metastases) see STAGING

TRANSITION: change; for example, the transition zone of the prostate is the area of the prostate closest to the urethra and has features which distinguish it from the much larger peripheral zone

TRANSPERINEAL: through the perineum

TRANSRECTAL: through the rectum

TRANSURETHRAL: through the urethra

TREATMENT: administration of remedies to a patient for a disease

TRUS: TRANSRECTAL ULTRASOUND; a method that uses echoes of ultrasound waves (far beyond the hearing range) to image the prostate by inserting an ultrasound probe into the rectum; commonly used to visualize prostate biopsy procedures

TRUS-P: see TRUS

TUMOR: an excessive growth of cells caused by uncontrolled and disorderly cell replacement; an abnormal tissue growth that can be either benign or malignant; See BENIGN, MALIGNANT

TURP: TRANSURETHRAL RESECTION OF THE PROSTATE; a surgical procedure to remove tissue obstructing the urethra; the technique involves the insertion of an instrument called a resectoscope into the penile urethra, and is intended to relieve obstruction of urine flow due to enlargement of the prostate

TUR/P: see TURP

ULTRASOUND: sound waves at a particular frequency (far beyond the hearing range) whose echoes bouncing off tissue can be used to image internal organs (e.g., a baby in the womb)

UNDERSTAGING: the assignment of an overly low clinical stage at initial diagnosis because of the difficulty of assessing the available information with accuracy (e.g., stage T2b as opposed to stage T3b)

UNIT: a surgical term for a pint (usually of blood)

URETER: an anatomical tube which drains urine from one of the two kidneys to the bladder

URETHRA: the tube that drains urine from the bladder through the prostate and out through the penis

URGENCY: the need to urinate very soon

URINARY SYSTEM: the group of organs and their interconnections that permits excess, filtered fluids to exit the body, including (in the male) the kidneys, the ureters, the bladder, the urethra, and the penis

UROLOGIST: a doctor trained first as a surgeon who specializes in disorders of the genitourinary system

UTI: URINARY TRACT INFECTION; an infection identifiable by the presence of bacteria (or theoretically viruses) in the urine; may be associated with fever or a burning sensation on urination

VAS DEFERENS: tube through which sperm travel from the testes to the prostate prior to ejaculation

VASECTOMY: operation to make a man sterile by cutting the vas deferens, thus preventing passage of sperm from the testes to the prostate

VESICLE: a small sac containing a biologically important fluid

WATCHFUL WAITING: active observation and regular monitoring of a patient without actual treatment

WHITMORE-JEWETT STAGING: see STAGING

X-ray: a type of high energy radiation that can be used at low levels to make images of the internal structures of the body and at high levels for radiation therapy

ZOLADEX: trade or brand name for goserelin acetate, a LHRH agonist

ZONE: part or area of an organ

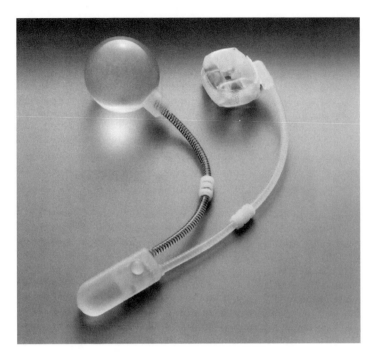

AMS Sphincter 800™ Urinary Prosthesis
Courtesy of American Medical Systems, Inc.
Minnetonka, Minnesota
Medical illustration by Michael Schenk

Acknowledgments

Many entries were taken with the generous permission of the following resources: Prostate Cancer InfoLink Dictionary, by Mike Scott, located at: http://www.comed.com/Prostate/Glossary html, Prostate Cancer Library, by Ron Koster:Glossary of PC Related Medical Terms, and Diagnostic and Staging Tests originated on the Prostate Cancer Bulletin Board on Prodigy and Steve Strum, M.D. Ed Piepmeier, May 1996 piepmeie@ccmail.orst.edu

Psalm 91, or my (Dennis) emergency Psalm 911
Just as my friend Bill underlined it before he knew that I had PCa.

Whoever goes to the Lord for safety, whoever remains under the protection of the Almighty can say to him," You are my defender and protector. You are my God; in you I trust."

He will keep you safe from all hidden dangers and from all deadly diseases. He will cover you with his wings, you will be safe in his care: his faithfulness will protect and defend you.

You need not fear any dangers at night or sudden attacks during the day or the plagues that strike in the dark or the evils that kill in daylight.

A thousand may fall dead beside you, ten thousand all around you, but you will not be harmed. You will look and see how the wicked are punished.

You have made the Lord your defender, the Most High your protector, and so no disaster will strike you, no violence will come near your home. God will put his angels in charge of you to protect you wherever you go.

They will hold you up with their hands to keep you from hurting your feet on the stones. You will trample down lions and snakes, fierce lions and poisonous snakes.

God says "I will save those who love me and will protect those who know me as Lord. When they call to me, I will answer them; when they are in trouble, I will be with them. I will rescue them and honor them. I will reward them with long life; I will save them."